I0836204

FOREIGN

REMINISCENCES,

BY

HENRY RICHARD

LORD HOLLAND.

EDITED BY HIS SON,

HENRY EDWARD LORD HOLLAND.

NEW YORK:
HARPER & BROTHERS, PUBLISHERS,
FRANKLIN SQUARE.
1855.

TO

JEROME BUONAPARTE,

MARSHAL OF FRANCE,

GOVERNOR OF THE "INVALIDES;"

THE ONLY SURVIVING BROTHER OF THE EMPEROR NAPOLEON;

This Work

IS RESPECTFULLY DEDICATED,

BY HIS GRATEFUL AND OBLIGED SERVANT,

HOLLAND.

Holland House, May 5, 1850.

PREFACE

THE recent events on the Continent have induced the Editor to publish the following pages on foreign politics. The times of which this volume treats have already acquired the interest of a long past age; and the public will read with pleasure, and perhaps with profit, the observations on passing events of a contemporary who, if not wholly impartial, is acknowledged by all who knew him to have been as candid as he was benevolent.

The Editor has scrupulously abstained from making the slightest verbal alteration in the text or notes. The omission of four insignificant sentences is all that he has deemed necessary for the immediate publication of what was probably written with the intention of not seeing the light so soon.

PARIS, *Sept.* 10, 1850.

FOREIGN REMINISCENCES.

A SHORT account, however desultory, of such persons, anecdotes, or political intrigues in foreign countries, as have fallen within my observation or knowledge, may not be uninteresting. But as a foreigner, however favorable his opportunities or sound his judgment, seldom relates any English event, or describes any English character, without committing some gross blunder, I check myself with the reflection that I also must be liable to be misled by false information, or to form an erroneous estimate of manners, opinions, and transactions out of my own country. I can only vouch for the anecdotes I record, by assuring my readers that I believe them; I repeat them as they were received and understood by me, from what appeared sufficient authority; and I delineate the characters either as the result of my own impressions, or of the opinions conveyed to me by those who were most capable of drawing them correctly.

In my first short journey abroad in 1791, I was a mere boy, and too little acquainted with the habits and language of the people among whom I was traveling to observe much, yet many interesting events were passing around me. I arrived at Paris not long after the death of Mirabeau, and soon after the acceptance of the constitution by Louis XVI. The designs of Mirabeau to coalesce with the court party, or at least to check the revolutionary spirit, were more than suspected before his death. He was in a constant state of intrigue with all parties, and particularly with Monsieur (Comte de Provence, and afterward Louis XVIII.) in the business of Favras. The Duke of Levi was the channel of communication between him and Monsieur in that mysterious and disgraceful affair. Yet the solicitude of the people during his illness was unabated, and stories almost incredible of the attention of the populace, in preventing the slightest disturbance in the street where he was lying ill, were related in all societies with that delight and admiration which dramatic displays of sentiment never fail to excite in Paris. The shops and quays were crowded with his portraits and busts. A stranger could discern in his physiognomy nothing but visible marks of debauch, vanity, presumption, and artifice, which were strong ingredients in his composition; but the Parisians, yet, stunned by his eloquence, and dazzled by his splendid talents, seemed to dwell on the representation of his large features, pock-fretted face, and frizzed hair, with fond complacency mingled with regret. He was certainly an extraordinary man. That his powers would have been equal, as has often been suggested, either to check or to guide the subsequent course of the French Revolution, may nevertheless be very questionable. He was thought to be, and probably was, very corrupt; but an exemption from that vice was the solitary virtue which gave individuals, and Robespierre in particular, any ascendency in the later and more stormy seasons of that frightful period.

Mirabeau had the talent, or at least the trick and contrivance, of appropriating the ideas and labors of other men to his purposes in a very extraordinary degree. I have been assured by one who knew him intimately,* and acted for a short time as his secretary, that not only the reports he made, but the speeches he delivered, were often written by others, and read by him in the morning, or even run through and adopted by him (as I have seen briefs by our lawyers) while he was actually speaking. The various imprisonments and embarrassments to which his disorderly life and licentious pen had exposed him are well known. The prosecution against him in England was the malevolent contrivance of a crazy and faithless servant, who falsely accused his master of having robbed him. There was nothing remarkable in that incident, but the public and warm testimony of Sir Gilbert Elliot and Mr. Burke himself in favor of a man whose influence on the French Revolution was afterward so conspicuous, and whose lax principles and immoral life furnished so fertile a theme for invectives against it. The vanity of Mirabeau exposed him,† it is said, to a droll reproof. At some im-

* This is my excellent friend Dumont; but, though he was veracious and fond of anecdotes, he was, by his own admission, a very inobservant, and, by my experience of him, a very credulous man.

† Though this anecdote was told me by many, and among them M. Dumont, I am disposed to question its accuracy; for M. Talleyrand, to whom the bon-mot was attributed, quarreled with Mirabeau upon the publication of the letters from Berlin, and never spoke to him afterward in private till a few days before his death, when Mirabeau

portant political crisis, he was descanting in society on the qualities requisite in a minister to extricate the crown, the assembly, and the nation from the difficulties in which they were involved, viz., great knowledge, great genius, acquaintance and perhaps connection with the upper ranks, some common feelings with the lower classes, a power of speaking and of writing eloquently and readily, familiarity with the world, the popularity of a martyr from recent prosecution, and many others, which it was obvious enough that he thought were united in himself. "All this is true," said a friend, "but you have omitted one of his qualities." "No—surely? what do you mean?" "Should he not," replied the same sarcastic friend, "be very much pitted with the small pox?"*

Mirabeau was not the only revolutionist supposed in 1791 to have been converted, or at least softened, toward the court. Barnave, touched (said the Royalists) by the behavior of the King and his family when he conducted them back from Varennes, disgusted and alarmed (said the Fayettists and Constitutionalists) by the coarse man-

sent for him, expressed his remorse at the publication, and prevailed upon Talleyrand to pronounce a posthumous speech composed by him (Mirabeau) on some subject then pending in the chamber. Moreover, I have discovered that my excellent friend Dumont, though veracity itself, was often *very credulous* about anecdotes recounted to him, and liable to mistakes about the dates, persons, and occasions. Yet when I asked Talleyrand, he did not entirely disdain the bon-mot: probably its excellence made it somewhat tempting to own it. Possibly he said it *of* and not *to* Mirabeau, in which case it is still good, but not so quick, clever, or striking.

* Et piqué de la petite vérole. It was Mirabeau's case to a very remarkable degree.

ners and bloody designs of the Jacobins, secretly seduced (whispered others) by the ambition of governing both parties in France, lent his very powerful aid to the more moderate councils, and contributed with Feuillans and Fayettists to prevent the establishment of a Republic, when the event seemed, if ever, to justify and recommend such a step. At the moment of the King's escape, that project must have occurred to many. It was checked even then by individuals among the Feuillans, and more particularly by D'André, a Provençal merchant, who, in spite of a strong accent, was a very able debater and popular leader in the Assembly, and who, through the gradations of a Feuillant, Fayettist, Constitutionalist, and Emigrant,* became ultimately an agent of the Bourbons, not without suspicion of having, at an earlier period, secretly connected himself with the designs of that family. He interrupted and overruled one Ramond, who was speaking to his Feuillant colleagues, the very day of the King's escape, on the necessity of a Republic, by touching his Provençal knife half in joke and half in earnest, and saying that he should use it against any one who seriously recommended the abolition of Monarchy. Lafayette assured me that, at a meeting of his friends, all present but two† agreed that

* He survived the restoration, returned to Paris, and was rewarded by the Bourbons, under whom he laid out and improved the Bois de Boulogne with much taste, judgment, and economy.

† Viz., the Duke de la Rochefoucault and Dupont de Nemours.

Lafayette, in speaking of the transactions of those days, many years afterward (January, 1826), assured me that he was surprised to find so many even of the most violent revolutionists concur in the notion of preserving monarchy after the arrest of the King. Some were for a

Monarchy must be, for a season at least, preserved; that France was not ripe for a Republic; and that a constitutional King was still necessary. The Duke de la Rochefoucault earnestly urged, before the others had spoken, the immediate declaration of a Republic, though, when it was otherwise decided, he never courted popularity, nor sought to distinguish himself from his friends by referring to such an opinion. On the contrary, he did his utmost to maintain the constitutional system, and the King at the head of it. The meeting alluded to occurred after the arrest at Varennes, and in the hotel of the Duke de la Rochefoucault. Surely the Duke de la Rochefoucault was in the right. The establishment of a Monarchy, with the view

change of dynasty. Wild men talked of the Duke of York, and Duke of Brunswick, and other foreign princes; perhaps some *thought more than they talked* of the Duke of Orleans; but the idea of a Republic was confined to a very few indeed, and even with republicans considered either as impracticable or premature. He added that many, and he among the number, were more readily inclined to acquiesce in the restoration of Louis XVI. from letters written by several English persons and particularly the Duchess of Devonshire and Mr. Fox, expressing great anxiety for his personal safety and that of the Queen. These letters they misinterpreted into an opinion of friendly but impartial spectators in favor of the preservation of monarchy in the person of Louis XVI. He acknowledged that he afterward learnt in conversation, that one of the letters at least, viz., that of Mr. Fox, was written with no such view, but simply from motives of humanity, and an ardent desire that the cause of the Revolution should not be sullied by any harsh or cruel proceeding against the individuals of the Royal Family. In other respects, Mr. Fox doubted of the policy and even of the justice of continuing Louis XVI. on the throne. I have heard him say that a separation of some years from the Queen should, in all prudence, have been stipulated as a condition.

of ripening it into a Republic, was as mischievous to the community as unjust to the Monarch; and the notion that Louis XVI. could become a constitutional King, disposed to weaken rather than strengthen his own authority, after his intended flight, and with the Queen for his consort and adviser, was chimerical and puerile in the extreme. He had justified his deposal by his flight. It was imprudent in Constitutionalists, it was madness in Republicans, not to insist on it. Above all, it was, as the event proved, very mistaken mercy.

Lafayette and others, however, from very generous motives, were averse to seizing such a moment for the subversion of Monarchy; and they were actively instrumental in discouraging all harshness, severity, or insolence to the King and his family. I dined frequently with General Lafayette. He kept a sort of open table for officers of the National Guard, and other persons zealous and forward in the cause of the Revolution. I was pleased with the unaffected dignity and simplicity of his manners, and flattered by the openness with which he spoke to me of his own views, and of the situation of the country. He was loud in condemning the brutality of Petion, whose cold and offensive replies to the questions of the royal prisoners on their journey back from Varennes were very currently reported; and he was in his professions, and I believe in his heart, much more confident of the sincerity of the King than common prudence should have allowed him to be, or than was justified either by the character of Louis himself, or by the truth as disclosed by subsequent events. Lafayette was, however, then as always, a pure, disinterested man, full of private affection and public virtue, and not devoid of such talents as firmness of purpose, sense of honor, and earnestness of zeal will, on great occasions, supply. He was indeed accessible to flattery, somewhat too credulous, and apt to mistake the forms, or, if I may so phrase it, the pedantry of liberty for the substance; as if men could not enjoy any freedom without subscribing to certain abstract principles and arbitrary tests, or as if the profession and subscription, nay, the technical observance of such tests and principles, were not, on the other hand, often compatible with practical oppression and tyranny. These strictures, however, on his blemishes are less applicable to the period to which I am now referring than to most others of his public life; for with all his love of popularity, he was then knowingly sacrificing it for the purpose of rescuing a court from contumely and injury, and, though a republican in principal, was active in preserving the name and perhaps too much of the authority of a King in the new constitution. He either tickled my youthful vanity, or gained my affections so much during my residence at Paris, that I caught his feelings, and became, for the time, enthusiastically persuaded of the King's sincere attachment to the new constitution. In this prepossession I was fortified by hearing his speech to the Legislative Assembly, which he delivered in a clear but tremulous voice, with great appearance of earnestness. Perhaps the qualified terms in which he acknowledged his original approbation and acceptance of the constitution gave greater force to the very positive assurances which he made that he would adhere to it. He seemed in his engagements for the future to be under no constraint, when he could so manifestly avow his reluctance to acquiesce in the past. "Enfin je l'ai acceptée et je la soutiendrai et dedans et dehors," are words which still ring on my ear, and which made no small impression at that time on my mind, not hitherto steeled, by experience of their hollowness, to royal speeches and written paragraphs. Louis XVI. was at that very moment, if not the main instigator, a coadjutor and adviser of the party soliciting foreign powers to put down that very constitution by force.* Louis XVI., however, was neither a bad nor a foolish man, and he certainly was not a cruel one. But sincerity is no attribute of princes educated in the expectation of power, and exposed to the dangers of civil disturbance. As Louis did not inherit, so neither did he acquire, that virtue by discipline or reflection. He meant the good of the people whom he deemed himself destined to govern, but he thought to promote that good more certainly by preserving than by surrendering any part of the authority which his ancestors possessed. Vanity,† a weed indigenous in the soil and

* It is just to observe that Lafayette, and some others concerned in the transactions of those days, even now acquit Louis XVI. of all participation in the plan of invading France; that I have no private knowledge on the subject whatever; and that my opinion and statement in the text are founded entirely on public and historical documents accessible to every one.

† I am aware that in imputing this vice to Louis XVI., I contradict not only a common report and tradition, but the testimony of many who had opportunities of studying his character. My opinion is founded on the evidence of facts, on the judgment and representation of M. de Calonne, confirmed by several traits related to me, without any view of maintaining any theory on the subject, by emigrants and courtiers, and by some circumstances in the Memoirs of Bezenval

much favored by an elevated state on which flattery is continually showered, confirmed that notion in his mind and disinclined him to any real confidence in his ostensible ministers and advisers. It made him fondly imagine that he never could become the tool of secret machinations, or the instrument of persons in his judgment so greatly inferior in intellect and acquirements, as those who surrounded him. M. de Calonne told me that when he had ascertained that the Queen and her coterie were hostile to the plans he had prepared, he waited on the King, respectfully and delicately lamented the Queen's reported disapprobation of his project, earnestly conjuring his Majesty, if not resolved to go through with the plan, and to silence all opposition, or cavil at it within the court, to allow him to suppress it in time; but if, on the other hand, his Majesty was determined to persevere, suggesting the propriety of impressing on the Queen his earnest desire and wishes that nothing should escape her lips which could sanction a doubt of the excellence of the measures themselves, and still less of the determination of the court to adopt and enforce them. Louis at first scouted the notion of the Queen (*une femme*, as he called her), forming or hazarding any opinion about it. But when M. de Calonne assured him that she spoke of the project in terms of disparagement and censure, the King rang the bell, sent for her Majesty to the apartment,

and *Madame Campan*, the latter of which, when divested of the decorum, not to say hypocrisy, with which such subjects must necessarily be treated by a lady attached to the court, will convince a reader who has a key to the secret, that Louis was in her judgment, self-sufficient in his disposition, disobliging, and even coarse and brutal in his manners.

and after sternly and even coarsely rebuking her for meddling with matters, *auxquelles les femmes n'ont rien à faire,* he, to the dismay of De Calonne, took her by the shoulders, and fairly turned her out of the room like a naughty child. "Me voilà perdu," said De Calonne to himself, and he was accordingly dismissed, and his scheme abandoned, in the course of a few days.*

Marie Antoinette did not obtain an ascendant over her husband in consequence of any such complexion in him as had brought his cousins of the Spanish branch so often under the dominion of their wives. Indeed, though the calumnies against the unhappy Queen were often atrociously unjust, it is perhaps fortunate for her reputation that the nature of the topic is sufficient to account for the silence of Madame Campan respecting the causes of that *tardiness* of affection in the king alluded to in her work. Had that lady † been released from the restraints which

* See Appendix, No. I.

† Madame Campan's delicacy and discretion are not only pardonable, but praiseworthy; but they are disingenuous, and her Memoirs conceal truths well-known to her, though such as would have been unbecoming a lady to reveal. She was, in fact, the confidante of Marie Antoinette's amours. Those amours were not numerous, scandalous, or degrading, but they *were amours.* Madame Campan, who lived beyond the restoration, was not so mysterious in conversation on these subjects as she is in her writings. She acknowledged to persons who have acknowledged it to me, that she was privy to the intercourse between the Queen and the Duc de Coigny. That French nobleman, from timidity of character and coldness of constitution, was not sorry to withdraw himself early from so dangerous an intrigue. Madame Campan confessed a curious fact, namely, that Ferson was in the Queen's boudoir or bed-chamber, *tête-à-tête* with her Majesty

the delicacy of her sex imposed on her relation, she might have found it difficult to reconcile a true exposition of the details with her avowed confidence in the virtue of Marie Antoinette, or at least to have persuaded men of professional experience, that the birth of the royal children was a proof and a triumph of surgical skill.

As I was not presented at court, I never saw the Queen but at the play-house. She was then in affliction, and her countenance was, no doubt, disfigured by long suffering and resentment. I should not, however, suppose that the habitual expression of it, even in happier seasons, had ever been very agreeable. Her beauty, however extolled, consisted, I suspect, exclusively in a fair skin, a straight person, and a stately air, which her admirers termed dignity, and her enemies pride and disdain. Her total want of judgment and temper no doubt contributed to the disasters of the Royal Family, but there was no member of it to whom the public was uniformly so harsh and unjust, and her trial and death were among the most revolting parts of the whole catastrophe. She was indeed insensible when led to the scaffold; but the previous persecution which she underwent was base, unmanly, cruel, and ungenerous to the last degree.

In 1792, the princes of the blood, with the exception of

on the famous night of the 6th of October. He escaped observation with considerable difficulty, in a disguise which she (Madame Campan herself) procured for him.

This, M. de Talleyrand, though generally somewhat averse to retailing anecdotes, disparaging of the Royal Family of France, has twice recounted to me, and assured me that he had it from Madame Campan herself.

the Duke of Orleans,* had left the country. I had known the Duke of Orleans slightly in England, and some of my friends and relations were acquainted, and in some senses were connected with him; but I saw little or nothing of him at Paris in 1791. He probably overlooked me, or if he did not, was unwilling to show civility to a stranger who frequented Lafayette, and who lived in a society particularly hostile to him. I regret not having seen more of him, because I believe that no man has lived in my time whose character has been more calumniated, or will be more misrepresented to posterity, and I should have liked to have confirmed or corrected this persuasion of mine by more personal observation than I had any opportunity of making. His carriage and countenance, though the latter was disfigured by carbuncles, *were* prepossessing, and his manners were perfect. His superiority in those respects, as well as his command of money, excited the jealousy of the court. His popularity at Paris, the *Judicium Paridis*, was perhaps sufficient to account for the first estrangement of the Queen, though some scandalous, but I really believe unfounded rumors would represent the other hemistich of Virgil's verse, the *spretæ injuria formæ*, or neglect of her advances, among the causes of that strong aversion which marked her language and conduct long before any political differences could have justified or explained such hatred. Many womanish artifices were resorted to to vex him, to spoil his amusements, to interrupt his parties, and to expose him to those small mortifications which, in all countries, are apt to awaken the resentment of weak minds as much or more

* The old Prince de Conti was, I believe, still in France, but too insignificant there and every where to require any notice.

than serious injuries, and to which an extravagant importance is always annexed in France, even by persons otherwise of some sense and magnanimity. That hostility, however, in which the court, *not the Duke of Orleans*, was the aggressor, was by no means confined to petty warfare. In defiance of decency and truth, the most malignant charges of cowardice were propagated and countenanced by the Queen and her party against the Duke of Orleans on his return from the fleet in 1778.* I have heard well-informed Frenchmen ascribe his visits to England and predilection for our usages, then termed *Anglomanie*, to the studious exclusion of him from both the business and the amusements of his native court, and to the disgust he felt at the direct and indirect slights put upon him. At the same time it must be acknowledged that his habits were far from respectable. Those † who had first engaged him in the Rev-

* This is not only asserted in the printed memoirs of Madame de Genlis, and by the uniform report of persons connected with the Palais Royal, but Talleyrand, Lafayette, Lord St. Helen's, Puysegur and other emigrant royalists, have admitted it to me in conversation frequently, and even borne their testimony to facts in corroboration of it. The malignity and falsehood of the charges against him are admitted by the author of the introduction to his correspondence (whoever he was), printed and published at Paris in 1800 in 8vo, by Le Rouge, imprimeur, and Debraye, bookseller, which publication confirms much besides in my text.

† Who were the individuals who swayed the politics of the Duke of Orleans, urged him on this occasion to return, and managed for him his interests and popularity with the rabble at Paris, is a mystery very difficult to penetrate. Madame de Genlis inflamed his animosity against the Queen, and, though she denied it, was certainly instrumental in originally immersing him and afterward maintaining him in

olution were dissatisfied at his absence in England, to which the remonstrances, and some pretend the actual menaces, of Lafayette, after the 6th of October, had driven him.* They considered it as a pusillanimous desertion, and incessantly urged him to quit a retirement which assumed the

political intrigues. Laclos, his secretary, was a man of great talent, much suspected, but never convicted of "close designs and crooked counsels." Siéyes, too, had influence with him. Ducrest, the brother of Madame Genlis, notwithstanding some disputes and lawsuits with the Duke of Orleans, is said to have had some influence with him, and to have uniformly exerted all he had against the court.

* Many, and some honorable men, had assured Lafayette that they actually saw the Duke of Orleans in the mob of the 6th of October. he afterward believed, and indeed knew, especially from M. Talleyrand that the fact was false, and the persons alleging it mistaken, yet the weight of the testimony at the time was so great that it, in his mind, overbalanced the mere improbability, and the representations to him to take some steps against the Duke of Orleans were so urgent that he determined to speak to him. They met at Madame de Coigny's. Lafayette advised him in a decided, perhaps somewhat peremptory tone to quit France, and insisted upon it "in a way (said Lafayette to me many years afterward), that if employed toward myself might, I must acknowledge, have had the effect of determining me to stay rather than go, yet it did not amount to a threat. He (Duke of Orleans) might show, by acting as he did upon it, some want of *moral courage*, but I had no right to imply (nor did I nor do I) any want of *personal courage* whatever. On the contrary, I do not believe that he was at all deficient in that quality, on that or on any other occasion." The ostensible reason of his journey was, as is well known, a mission on the affairs of Belgium, and he certainly endeavored, though without success, to render that mission more than a pretext. In his letters published at Paris in 1800, see note of 3d of April, 1790, p. 120. Correspondence de Louis Philippe, Duc d' Orleans, chez Le Rouge et Debraye, Paris, 1800.

appearance of an ignominious, though voluntary exile. To those remonstrances he reluctantly yielded, though if the court would have been prevailed upon to appoint him embassador in London, he distinctly offered to remain. Admiral Payne, who conducted him in a small boat to his yacht off Brighton, assured me that the Duke of Orleans, on taking leave, grasped his hand with much emotion, and, with tears in his eyes, said: "If I consulted my inclination or my safety I should stay in your happy country, but I am told that I am bound in honor to return; for that reason, and that reason only, I go. You, my dear Payne,* will recollect that I am not blind to my situation, nor to the scenes I am going to encounter. I shall do no good to any body, I shall lead a dreadful life, and I shall probably perish among the first, or, at least, very soon." Before leaving France, he had made some very slight advances to the court, but such as showed that if he and his friends had been secured from persecution and revenge by being admitted into a due share of power, he was not unwilling to co-operate in preventing matters from coming to extremities. He renewed these offers when in England, and before his return. He proposed and even solicited to have his pretended mission converted into a real embassy

* Admiral Payne, it must be acknowledged, had not the reputation of being very correct in his recital of stories, but I see no motive he could have for inventing this conversation; and the general impression I received of the Duke of Orleans' feelings at that period from Francis Duke of Bedford to whom he spoke in a similar strain at Woburn, as well as his language and conduct afterward, convince me that in substance this relation is true, and that the words put into the mouth of that ill-fated Prince on his departure from England contain an accurate representation of his sentiments.

to London, but when refused by M. Montmorin, he seems to have considered (and surely not very unnaturally) the exhortation not to return, and the reasons assigned for it, namely, that his presence might aggravate the turbulence and difficulty of the times, as an insult rather than an encouragement. Far from preventing, it provoked his return to Paris. He met on that, and every other occasion, nothing but repulse, disdain, and insult from the courtiers. This might be very fine and magnanimous, but was very impolitic withal. If it does not justify, it at least somewhat palliates, and very satisfactorily accounts for his subsequent connection with more violent councils. After the return of the King from Varennes, it is said* that he declined the Presidentship, and was unwilling to take any forward part. Some attribute that backwardness to hypocrisy and others to pusillanimity. But if the fact be as it is stated, is it clear that delicacy toward the royal prisoners, and an unaffected reluctance to be forced into a station of power, were not among the real motives for his forbearance? Surely that was the opportunity, which a man of the unprincipled ambition and thirst of vengeance so often imputed to him would have chosen for activity! The construction I am disposed to put upon his conduct is as follows: Popularity and some triumph over the malignity of the court, especially of the Queen, were naturally enough his objects at the beginning of the Revolution: he soon grew tired of the intrigues, then shocked at the excesses, and at last alarmed at the consequences of that event; and before the time I am now referring to, 1791, his own ease and safety, and

* In various publications, but I do not vouch for the fact.

the protection of such as had incurred any enmities on his account, was all that he expected, or perhaps as much as he wished to obtain. Talleyrand, who knew him well, and who in a joint work with Beaumetz, which was never published, shortly afterward delineated his character, described him to me as indifferent alike to the pursuits of pleasure or vanity, ambition or revenge, and solely intent on enjoying ease and preserving existence. He was so jaded (*si blasé, un homme si désabusé*), that he had outlived even the necessity of emotion (*le besoin de s'émouvoir*). There is, indeed, reason to suspect that the persons instrumental in creating and preserving his personal influence in Paris, were active agents in the municipal cabals and revolutions which preceded and accompanied the 10th of August and the 2d of September of 1792; and true it is, that the only party which showed the least disposition to identify itself with his interests, or to concert with him, consisted of a portion of those to whose language and manœuvres the horrors even of that last day are mainly attributed by well informed authors. Some of them, and Danton in particular,* were not unwilling in concert with the Duke of

* Danton, who is well known to have been an unprincipled, corrupt, and dauntless man, was alternately in communication with all parties, and was employed, if not bribed by the court, to use every means to impair the popularity of Lafayette and the Constitutionalisis. He received 4000 louis from Montmorin, probably for that purpose. Lafayette, who had ascertained the fact, upbraided Danton with it in one of the few interviews he had with him, to dissuade him from instigating the mob to insults on the Royal Family in 1792. Danton acknowledged the receipt of the money, but called it an indemnity for a place of *Avoué*, which he had lost by a decree of the Constituent Assembly. It was probably on the occasion of that payment, and his subsequent conduct

Orleans to save the life of the King, and by a junction with the Brissotins and moderate Republicans, to put a stop to the excesses of the populace, provided *they could obtain an oblivion and impunity for all that had hitherto passed.* But Republicans and philosophers were as unreasonably hostile and nearly as blindly improvident wherever the Duke of Orleans was concerned, as the Royalists themselves. Scruples, honorable no doubt, but highly unseasonable, and not altogether consistent with their own conduct before and during the 10th of August, made the friends of Roland, Brissot, and Gaudet, ıevolt at any thing like coalition with men covered with the blood of their fellow-citizens, though such a junction was the obvious,

so little in unison with the opinion of those from whom he received it, that he made the impudent defense imputed to him: "On donne volontiers 80,000 francs pour une homme comme moi, mais on n'a pas un homme comme moi pour 80,000 francs." In the same conversation with Lafayette, he told that General that he was more of a *Royalist* than he was, which, as Lafayette observed was not difficult to be, but no reason for treating Royality with brutality and insult. The fact, however, is that the more one ascertains of the conduct of Danton, by far the ablest, though the most corrupt of all the Terrorists of 1792, the more ground one finds for suspecting that he had some designs, and even some principle, though not favorable to the monarchy. He would, no doubt, have preferred from obvious and personal motives (as many honest men would have done for public and patriotic reasons), an indirect dynasty in the house of Orleans to a direct one in that of Louis XVI. or XVII.; all persons who combine a love of freedom with a sense of the necessity of monarchy, must acknowledge that in England a Nassau or a Brunswick was preferable to a Stuart; and that in France a Bonaparte or an Orleans is much more reconcilable with safe and free government than a prince whose title is exclusively derived from primogeniture and lineal descent.

and perhaps the solitary, method of preventing the effusion of more. Danton and his followers, who had so largely participated in the crimes of the Terrorists, were compelled to proceed with their associates, when they despaired of obtaining impunity from the triumph of the more moderate and numerous but less popular party in the Convention. The Duke of Orleans could not have saved the King by voting against his death; and he more certainly than any one man in the assembly would have accelerated his own by so doing. On the other hand, he was also the one man in that assembly, on whom, had any counter-revolution occurred, the Royal vengeance would most unquestionably have fallen without mercy. Such considerations would not weigh with a Cato, but they were calculated to shake the constancy of ordinary men. The Duke of Orleans had, therefore, at least as much excuse for the vote he gave as the 360 who voted with him; and those who hold regicide to be the greatest of possible crimes, have nevertheless no right to select him as the greatest criminal. He was well aware of the peculiarity of his own situation. Of that I have seen some curious proofs in a short narrative written by Mrs. Elliott, who had, I believe, lived with him, and who, on the score of old acquaintance, prevailed on him to save, through his garden at Monceaux, and at no small peril to himself, the younger Chancency,* who was implicated in the affair of the 10th of August, and who, as was justly observed by the Duke in his hearing, so far from incurring any risk to

* He took the name of Quintin, together with an estate in Yorkshire; and on the restoration of Louis XVIII. held an office of rank in the Tuileries.

serve him, would have been among the first to urge his execution. He was, to my knowledge, among the last to relieve the subsequent distresses of his generous benefactress, Mrs. Elliott, or to mitigate the censures with which it was the fashion in most companies throughout Europe to visit the name of the Duke of Orleans. That Prince perished soon afterward on the scaffold, and disproved one of the imputations cast upon him, by the composure with which he met his fate.*

It was in this visit to Paris in 1791, that I first formed acquaintance with M. Talleyrand. I have seen him in most of his vicissitudes of fortune; from his conversation I have derived much of the little knowledge I possess of the leading characters in France before and during the Revolution. He was then still a bishop. He had, I believe, been originally forced into holy orders, in consequence of his lameness, by his family, who, on that account, treated him with an indifference and unkindness shameful and shocking. He was for some time *aumonier* to his uncle, the Archbishop of Rheims; and when Mr. Pitt went to that town to learn French, after the peace of 1782, he lodged him in an apartment in the Abbey of St. Thierry, where he was then residing with his uncle, and constantly accompanied him for six weeks, a circumstance to which, as I have heard M. Talleyrand remark with some asperity, Mr. Pitt never had the grace to allude either during his embassy, or his emigration, or in 1794, when he refused to recall the cruel order by which he was sent away from England, under the alien bill. Talleyrand

* See Introduction à la Correspondance. Paris, 1800. Page iv. misprinted vi.

was initiated into public affairs under M. de Calonne, and learnt from that lively minister the happy facility of transacting business without effort and without ceremony in the corner of a drawing-room, or in the recess of a window. In the exercise of that talent, he equaled the readiness and surpassed the wit of his model, but he brought to his work some commodities, which the latter could never supply; viz., great veracity, discretion, and foresight. He displayed little or no talent for public speaking in the National Assembly. His reports and papers, especially one on education, procured him some celebrity, but were, I suspect, the composition of other men. His abilities were, however, acknowledged, for they were undeniable, and his future success foreseen. Of his joint embassy with M. Chauvelin, I have spoken elsewhere. He escaped from Paris five days after the 2d of September, with a passport from Danton, the grandee of democracy (*ce grand Seigneur de la Sansculotterie*, as Garat happily termed him). And he acknowledged that the passport was not only useful to his immediate object, but became yet more eminently so, when he was anxious to return to France under the Directory. It proved he was no emigrant. I had here related the interview between Danton and Talleyrand, in which the latter had obtained his passport, as I heard it soon after the event from Dumont,* to

* Dumont, as I have elsewhere remarked, was almost always unobservant and often inaccurate, though honest. My general and long observation of Talleyrand's veracity in great and small matters makes me confident his relation is correct. He may, as much or more than other diplomats, suppress what is true; I am quite satisfied he never actually says what is false, though he may occasionally imply it.

whom I thought Talleyrand had told it; but Talleyrand assured me (in 1830) that the passport did not cost him a shilling, and that Danton attempted neither to cheat nor to bully him; on the contrary, that he was obliging and even friendly. He gave a very diverting account of the reasons which induced him to be so, and it was manifest from his manner of recounting the scene that he had written it down. It forms most probably a passage in his memoirs, but is in character and complexion very different, and indeed almost the reverse of that which I had heard and recorded, but have now erased. It is possible that the circumstances I had attributed to Talleyrand's escape from Paris in 1792, had occurred between some other person and Danton, and that I or my informant had affixed the wrong name. He lived in England very frugally, in Kensington-square; he sold his library, and he was on the point of engaging with a bookseller to publish memoirs in concert with the ex-President Beaumetz, a gentleman of some literary acquirements. They had written a life of the Duke of Orleans. The facts and remarks were no doubt chiefly furnished by Talleyrand, but Beaumetz was said to have contributed the style and method of the composition. Talleyrand, however, bethought himself of the possibility of a return to France, and of the disadvantage to which a printed work of the kind might expose him. Beaumetz consented to suppress the publication, but the MS. probably remained with Talleyrand. Within these few years he has spoken to me of his memoirs, and read portions of them to friends of mine. It is remarkable that the passages and phrases frequently quoted with praise, are such as relate to the same period as the joint performance of him and M. Beaumetz in 1793.* Talleyrand disliked his residence in North America extremely. A curious paper written or dictated by him in the transactions of the Institute, records his opinion that the United States must ultimately connect themselves with the country from which they sprang, rather than with that to which they in some measure owe their independence. It is generally thought that he negotiated his return to France through Madame de Staël. He was on intimate terms with her, but had abandoned her society for that of Madame Grand† before the peace of 1802. when I saw him

* He has since read some relating to his very early life to me and Lady Holland and Allen, in which Beaumetz could have no share. They are admirable in style, as well as in sense. (1832.)

† "Il faut avoir aimé Madame de Staël pour connoître tout le bonheur d'aimer une bête," was a saying of his much quoted at Paris at that time, in explanation of his passion for Madame Grand, who certainly did not win him or any one else by the fascination of her wit or conversation. For thirty or forty years, the bon-mots of M. de Talleyrand were more frequently repeated and more generally admired than those of any living man. The reason was obvious. Few men uttered so many, and yet fewer any equally good. By a happy combination of neatness in language and ease and suavity of manner, with archness and sagacity of thought, his sarcasms assumed a garb at once so courtly and so careless, that they often diverted almost as much as they could mortify even their immediate objects. His humorous reproof to a gentleman vaunting with self-complacency the extreme beauty of his mother, and apparently implying that it might account for advantages in person in her descendants, is well known: "C'était donc," said he, "Monsieur votre père qui n'était pas si bien." The following is more recent, but the humor of it hardly less arch or less refined. The celebrity of M. de Chateaubriand, the vainest of mortals, was on the wane. About the same time, it happened to be casually

again at Paris. It became necessary on the conclusion of the *Concordat*, that he should either revert to the habits and character of a prelate, or receive a dispensation from all the duties and obligations of the order. He chose the latter. But Bonaparte, who affected at that time to restore great decorum in his consular court, somewhat maliciously insisted either on the dismissal of Madame Grand or his public nuptials with that lady. The questionable nature of her divorce from Mr. Grand created some obstacle to such a union. It was curious to see Sir Elijah Impey, the judge who had granted her husband damages in India for her infidelity, caressed at her little Court at Neuilly. His testimony was deemed essential, and he was not disposed to withhold it, because, notwithstanding his denial of riches in the House of Commons, he was at that very time urging a claim on the French Government to indemnify him for his losses in their funds. Mr. (Sir Philip) Francis her paramour, then at Paris also, did not fail to draw the attention of Englishmen to the circumstance, though he was not himself admitted at Neuilly to complete the curious group with his judicial enemy and quondam mistress. M. de Calonne at the same period came to France on the plea of private affairs; but with equal levity, presumption, and talent he contrived to ingratiate himself with some of the most jacobinical ministers of the Consul. He had even concerted a plan with Fouché for supplanting Talleyrand and improving the financial system of Bonaparte. He introduced me to Fouché, whose countenance, manner, and

mentioned in conversation that Chateaubriand was affected with deafness, and complained bitterly of that infirmity. "Je comprends," said Talleyrand; "depuis qu'on a cessé de parler de lui il se croit sourd."

conversation exhibited at that time the profligacy and ferocity, the energy and restlessness which one might well expect to find blended in the character of a revolutionist, and which, though more carefully concealed when he became a courtier, were the chief ingredients in the composition of that vain and unprincipled tool of the Republic, the Consul, and the Bourbons. Talleyrand baffled his intrigue with the ex-minister of Louis XVI. The paper on finance written by Calonne, and delivered by the regicide minister of police to the Consul, was answered in the next Moniteur by the Consul himself, and the author, without being actually named, scornfully designated and bitterly ridiculed and reviled. I heard Talleyrand banter his old friend Calonne on his love of retreat, the night before he was compelled to quit Paris, and when Talleyrand possibly was aware that the order for his departure was actually signed.* He was, however, by the clemency of the Consul and the remembrance of old friendship in Talleyrand, allowed to return to Paris shortly afterward, and immediately on his arrival he died of a pleurisy and a bad physician, to whom when he could speak no longer, he wrote in pencil these remarkable words: *Tu m'as assassiné, et si tu es honnête homme, tu renonceras à la médecine pour jamais.* This

* Talleyrand assured me in 1830, that he did not know of the order to Calonne to quit Paris till after he had left it; but it is very possible that he had forgotten so trifling a circumstance; and if he did not, his expression to Calonne, "comment, Calonne, tu aimes donc la retrait?" *which I heard,* was an odd coincidence. He recollected distinctly Bonaparte's disgust at Fouché's protection of Calonne, and his contrasting it with the interest Barthelemy felt and expressed about Breteuil. "Barthelemy et Breteuil, celà est dans l'ordre des choses," said he, "mais Fouché et Calonne; ah fi donc! c'est de l'intrigue."

agreeable and remarkable man had long ceased to have any influence on public affairs. He was not only dismissed from office, and an emigrant from his country, but he was discarded from the council of the French Princes, to whom he had unnecessarily sacrificed his own and much of his wife's fortune before I knew him. I lived much with him during the last three years of his residence in England. He is one of the few public men whose character seems to me to have been well understood and faithfully drawn by the writers of the day. Easy, obliging, friendly, sprightly, and communicative in the intercourse of society, and singularly perspicuous in the statement as well as transaction of business, he had a levity of character, an imprudence in conversation and conduct, and I am afraid I must add a disregard of truth, and not unfrequently an ignorance on the subjects about which he talked confidently and eloquently, which seemed almost incredible in a person ambitious of acting a part in the affairs of the world, and actually employed in situations of great importance. Though exiled before the Revolution, and not insensible to the ill-treatment he had received from the court, he gallantly and incautiously devoted his time and fortune to the service of the emigrant Princes. He was commissioned by them to solicit the aid of the various sovereigns in Europe and particularly of Leopold, who had recently become Emperor of Germany, and who communicated through various private and ill-chosen channels with Calonne, traveling under the feigned name of an English gentleman, at Florence. His private assurances were not in Calonne's estimation much more encouraging than the cold, reserved, and ambiguous papers which, during his short reign, issued from the court of Vienna on the subject of the French Revolution. Indeed, according to M. de Calonne, the royal emigrants had little reason to be satisfied with any of the sovereigns of that period, except the Kings of Sweden and Prussia,* both of whom espoused

* The *Mémoires d'un Homme d'Etat* published at Paris in 1828, and said to be either written by the Prussian minister Hardenberg, or made up from papers he had left, agree in many particulars with the impressions, views, and recollections I have here recorded. I had written this and other passages relating to the war of Prussia against France of 1792, before I read the *Mémoires d'un Homme d'Etat.* Of the authenticity of that work I know nothing, but its explanations of events of that day tally singularly with some points of information which I collected from French and Prussian individuals, and which differ from the common reports of these matters. According to the author of that work, Gustavus was the only king disposed to head the emigrants in a crusade against France, with or without the assistance of other sovereigns. Catharine was as earnest in persuading him and others to undertake it, and Frederick William as sincerely desirous of engaging his brother sovereigns in the design, without any sinister views of aggrandizement or dismemberment. But he was at first cajoled by Leopold, then imperceptibly swayed by his cabinet and generals, and ultimately galled and provoked by the selfish duplicity of Austria. Calonne's version of the matter to me did not materially differ from this. He did not indeed mark the shades between Gustavus and Frederick William, or dwell on the epoch before the death of the former, when the latter was, from prudence and from deference to Leopold, comparatively cold to the Princes and emigrants, nor did he mark so broadly the discrepancy between the secret communication of the court of Versailles (including the Queen) to the coalesced sovereigns, and those of the Princes and emigrants, as the author of the Mémoires. But he, in the main, described Leopold as irresolute, selfish, and averse to the cause as well as to the emigrants, and Frederick William as originally earnest, sincere, and disinterested, but afterward a little perverted and much disgusted.

the cause cordially, and from a conviction that it was the interest of crowned heads to extinguish the revolutionary principles then prevalent in France. Gustavus III., a man of more cunning than wisdom, and more ambition than courage, but not destitute of talents, was soon afterward murdered. Frederick William, became by a strange fatality of circumstances, the chief deserter and betrayer of that monarchical confederacy, of which he was originally the most earnest, and perhaps throughout the least insincere member. I spent the summer and autumn of 1792 in Denmark and Prussia. In both those countries I was struck with two circumstances in the state of public opinion, which account for many subsequent events in Europe, though the impression made by those events has obliterated with many the recollection of former feelings, and produced such changes as may invalidate with posterity the credibility of my testimony to their existence. The first was the universal persuasion that France would be subdued; the second, the general dissatisfaction and pain with which the prospect of such success was contemplated by large classes of the people.

Military men, politicians, and all who were styled *good company*, treated any resistance to regular German armies by French troops, much more by National Guards, raw levies, volunteers, or peasantry, as an utter impossibility. The art of war, said they, was reduced to a certainty; the notion of valor, enthusiasm, or numbers defeating disciplined troops, commanded by an experienced captain like the Duke of Brunswick, was as chimerical as an attempt to confute a problem in mathematics by metaphor, fancy, or ingenuity. Moreover, the moral as well as the scientific superiority of the military powers (for so the German courts then termed themselves κατ' ἐξοχην) over Frenchmen, was equally insisted upon. The battle of Rosbach was in every mouth. But though such was the expectation of success, there was not equal joy at the prospect of it. Many military characters of high name, particularly in Prussia, deprecated the policy of the war, as tending to aggrandize Austria; and the people throughout the Protestant countries of the North obviously wished, though they dared not hope, success to Revolutionary France. Neither was the great mass of the mercantile and literary world at much pains to conceal their alarm at the approaching triumph of royalty, aristocracy, and military authority over those principles of equality, which in their judgment tended to promote the industry, improve the faculties, and better the condition of mankind. Such considerations preserved, for a long period, the little kingdom of Denmark, under the prudent guidance of the minister Bernstorff, in a state of perfect neutrality, notwithstanding a childish disposition in the Crown Prince to ape the great King of Prussia, and notwithstanding the exhortations and menaces of the various members of the confederacy and the influence which one of them must always possess in the councils of the court of Copenhagen.

The Crown Prince (afterward Frederick VI.), nephew of our king, was the ostensible head of the government. The incapacity of his father was acknowledged, and though he continued to sign the edicts and public instruments, he was not permitted to take any part in the deliberation upon them, nor were any of his acts deemed valid, unless countersigned by his son, whom the council had in truth invested with all the functions of royal authority. In fact the royal signature was preserved as a medical rather than political expedient. The object was to humor and soothe the feelings of the deposed monarch, not to give any validity to acts which, without reference to such formality, were recognized by the courts of justice, and obeyed by the people. When first set aside, he had bitterly wept at being no longer a king, and adduced as a proof of the misfortune which had befallen him, that he had no longer any papers to sign. To satisfy him, they were afterward offered him for signature, and he never declined annexing his name to all that were presented to him, from a fear of losing that, his sole remaining, but, in his view, distinctive prerogative of royalty. It happened once or twice, from some motive of convenience or accident, that the Crown Prince put his name to an instrument, before it was sent to his royal father for his signature; the jealous old monarch perceived it, and when the next paper was brought, he, to the surprise and consternation of the courtiers, signed "Christian and Co^{nia}," maliciously observing, that he was once sole proprietor of his firm, but he found it was now a partnership, and would spare his associates the trouble of adding their names. His insanity was throughout of a playful rather than a malignant nature. When it was the policy of the Queen Dowager, his step-mother, to maintain him in the exercise of his functions, she used to exhibit him at card parties in public. It is usual in the north of Europe to score with chalk, but his Majesty on such occasions diverted himself with employing it in a less decorous manner. He would draw the most obscene figures on the green baize, and wink to the by-standers whenever the Queen Dowager, with an averted face and affected carelessness, rubbed out the obnoxious representations with her cards, her hands, her handkerchief, a napkin, or any thing which she could, with some appearance of absence, pass over them for that purpose. He continued for many years to dine occasionally in public. Though the foreign ministers were cautioned neither to provoke, nor to remark any of his peculiarities, he not unfrequently succeeded in disconcerting them. He would, for instance, ask them to drink wine, and then throw the contents of his glass in the face of the page behind him, and when by this, and the addition of sundry grimaces, gesticulations and antics, he had provoked a smile, he would suddenly assume a grave and solemn countenance, and addressing the minister opposite say, "Monsieur l'envoyé parait fort gai? y a-t-il quelque chose qui l'amuse?—je le prie de m'en faire part." Such was the innocent nature of the royal insanity. It is a satire or a commendation on the institution of monarchy to remark that under this absolute Prince, whose childishness amounted to imbecility and lunacy, the commerce, agriculture and prosperity of the kingdom continued to improve, the people were relieved from the ancient feudal burdens which oppressed them, tranquillity was preserved, justice purely and impartially administered, and even the foreign policy conducted throughout a period of unexampled peril and confusion in Europe, in a manner which, when the insignificant resources of Denmark are considered, must be acknowledged to be creditable and even glorious. That little state of Denmark seems indeed an exception to all rules. An arbitrary monarchy established with the consent, nay, at the tumultuous instance of the people, has continued for more than a century to be administered with prudence, wisdom, and moderation. During a large portion of that time, her prime ministers have been selected from one and the same family, not only of foreign birth and extraction, but never identified in interest with the nation they governed, by the purchase or inheritance of any land within its territories. The Bernstorffs were all Germans, and their estates as well as their purchases were all in Germany. The actual representative of the family,* himself for some time minister in Denmark, has returned to his native country, and presides over foreign affairs at Berlin. His uncle was in office when I was in Copenhagen. He was a man of enlightened understanding, agreeable manners, and benevolent disposition.

If the language of the diplomatic corps at that court and at Hamburgh and Berlin in 1792, corresponded with the real sentiments of their respective governments, the neutral as well as the belligerent Powers of Europe had as little pretension to the praise of moderation in views, scruple in their means, or humanity in their feelings as the French Revolutionists; and the expression of their principles was always as unqualified and not unfrequently as coarse, vulgar, and unmannerly as that of the Sansculotte demagogues at Paris. Count Bernstorff, indeed, never sanctioned or encouraged any of the extravagant professions of what was called loyalty and regular government at that period. That prudence preserved the dignity of his character, and spared him many mortifications. Whenever policy or necessity brought him in contact with the ministers and agents of the various governments of France, he had neither to retract, explain, nor deny any opinion that he had privately

* 1826.

or publicly expressed, a humiliation to which almost every prince or public man throughout Europe was exposed and submitted, in the course of the ensuing twenty years, thus betraying a pliancy of principle, for which history will withhold from their excesses in prosperity the honorable excuse of fanaticism, and from their sufferings in adversity the grace and dignity of martyrdom. In continuance of the singular contrast subsisting between the results and the ingredients of the Danish monarchy, their affairs have been very prosperously conducted under their present king, Frederick VI., then Crown Prince. Yet, he was and is a person of mediocrity, with few natural advantages, and generally more known for weaknesses, such as drunkenness and vanity, than distinguished for any qualifications of a commanding nature. One anecdote, if true, would seem to prove that he was not devoid of shrewd observation and sly humor. He was at Vienna during the Congress of 1814. Wherever in the treaties there negotiated there had been a fresh distribution of territories, and in the German and adjoining States there had been many, the value of each cession respectively was estimated by the number of inhabitants, and in diplomatic language the cession was described as that of so many souls, or *ames*. Now there was no accession of territory to Denmark, but, on the contrary, some small diminution. The King was much courted during the negotiations, and treated with friendly cordiality and personal friendship by the Emperor of Austria. That high personage, on his taking leave, complimented him most warmly on his attainments and good conduct, and the golden opinion they had acquired. "Pendant votre séjour ici (said he), votre Majesté a gagné tous les cœurs."

"Mais *pas une seule ame*," replied somewhat causticly the ill-requited sovereign of a well-governed people. Till then he was never suspected of being alive to the mortifications he had received, and still less of being capable of recording his sense of them, by so smart and well-merited a repartee.

As the King of Prussia* and his sons were with the army, I saw nothing of the court, and little of the leading men at Berlin, in 1791. Alversleben and the other ministers were mere ciphers, or, at the best, such men of form and business as are the "common growth of courts." General Moellendorf, at whose table I dined once or twice, was remarkable for his personal appearance, which was that of a frank, bold, and athletic veteran, for being one of the most distinguished captains of the Great Frederick's school, and for his undisguised disapprobation of the war with France. He was the pattern of an old German general; and his dinner, which lasted many hours, a specimen of the old-fashioned banquets of that country. The Queen Dowager, widow of Frederick, was superannuated and unintelligible; and the reigning Queen who mistook me for Lord Holderness, and asked me if I had not accompanied the Princess Mary to Hesse Castle in 1746, was nearly crazy. The courts of Princess Henry and Prince Ferdinand at Bellevue alone contributed to the society of the place. The Princess Henry was a stiff, uninteresting, but hospitable personage, who lived separate from her husband, and received in a stately formal manner natives and foreigners twice during the week. The etiquette established by Frederick, in consequence of some uncourtly

* Frederick William II.

repartees from foreign ministers, and, I believe, from Mr. Hugh Elliot in particular, was still in full force; and, whenever a royal personage sat down to table, all the diplomatic corps were obliged to retire. The exclusion did not extend to foreigners who had no employment: it was rather a whimsical exhibition to observe our minister, and other diplomats, start like guilty things, and withdraw, as the organ in the German clock of her Royal Highness's apartment began to summon us with a tune to supper, at eleven. Prince Henry was at that time at Rheinsberg; where, some years afterward, I visited him with my family. His aversion to the war was attributed to predilection for France and Frenchmen, and to rivalry and jealousy of the Duke of Brunswick, to whom the command of the army had been intrusted by the King. He was so partial to every thing French, that he had not only a troop of French comedians in his palace, but studiously confined his reading and his conversation to that language. Indeed, he had either forgotten his native tongue so entirely, or affected to speak it so ill, that, when with unexpected condescension he directed the postillions by what road to drive me to Potsdam, they actually laughed in his face at his defective and foreign pronunciation of the words. But his many private peculiarities, as well as his military and political actions, are recorded in various histories and memoirs, and his character is admirably, though somewhat roughly drawn, in the celebrated letters of Mirabeau, from Berlin. He was the ablest of the three brothers of Frederick; and, if inferior to him in the field and in the cabinet, was less forgetful of his friends, less unforgiving to his enemies, and in all respects less selfish and unfeeling than that extraordinary but unprincipled man. He had been deeply affected at the treatment of his brother Augustus;* he told me that he had at one time recorded the truth in his memoirs, and vindicated the memory of that prince by exposing the cruelty and injustice of the King; but that the latter, having either suspected or ascertained his intentions, had adroitly sealed his mouth, and compelled him to suppress the passage, by extolling him (Prince Henry), in his "History of the Seven Years' War," so warmly, and so much beyond his deserts, that he should incur the imputation of the basest ingratitude if he left any memorial of the weakness or wickedness of his encomiast behind him. He raised, however, a monument in his garden, with a long inscription, to the honor of his less fortunate brother, and he had the spirit to open and to illuminate it on the festival which he gave on the occasion of the King's visit to Rheinsberg. He left his opinions on the war of 1792 to be inferred from the language held at Bellevue, the villa of his brother, Prince Ferdinand. There the campaign was very freely canvassed, the French generals extolled, and the conduct even of the Convention, the clubs, and the Jacobins not unfrequently palliated. The daughter of that house, Princess Louisa (afterward Princess Radzivil), was a remarkable person: according to rumor, she had been educated with the hopes of marrying the Prince of Wales. She had unquestionably studied with success the language and usages of England. It is said that George III. object-

* Called, I think, Prince Royal, and father of Frederick William II. He is supposed to have died of a broken heart after the battle of Kolin, in consequence of the cold reception and the unqualified censures with which the King resented his failure in that campaign.

ed to any union with that branch of the house of Brandenburgh, with an observation drawn from the scandalous chronicle of Berlin, viz., that none of his children should ally themselves "with the children of Schmettau."* Frederick, when there was not much prospect of an heir in the other branches, had placed a distinguished officer of engineers of that name in the family of his brother Ferdinand, in the hope and expectation, and, perhaps, with the express injunction, that he would supply all deficiencies in the household. The Princess, though lofty and decorous in her demeanor, was not long insensible to the personal and mental charms of her chamberlain; and Schmettau annually announced the birth of a prince, and received some handsome presents for the good news; till, on the third visit, according to Mirabeau, the King, after giving him a gold-headed cane, called him back and said, "*Schmettau, trois! c'est assez.*" Such anecdotes, very currently related, raised a smile every where else, but serious scruples in the mind of George III. Had he, however, been as consistent in them as in most others, he would have objected to another alliance of his family with the house of Brandenburgh. The exiled and divorced Queen of Prussia† is much belied, if, on the marriage of her daughter with the Duke of York, she did not observe to the chamberlain who announced it, that it was a good match enough for the daughter of Müller the musician, one whom she was accused of admitting to criminal familiarities. Her

* Aux enfans de Schmettau.

† I should have said wife of Frederick William, for I believe he had divorced her, and married again, before he succeeded to the Crown.

husband himself, at one time sanctioned the conjecture. With the view of debauching the young Princess, his reputed daughter, he endeavored, but in vain, to lessen her abhorrence of any compliance with his passion, by depriving it of the aggravation of incest, and disclaiming all pretensions of being her father. Such disgusting profligacy should seldom be recorded: I would not defile this narrative with such impurities if I did not know, from the best authority, that what I relate is true; and if I did not think it useful and right to expose the state of manners in those German courts, which, with an hypocrisy as revolting as their vices, alleged a dread of the subversion of religion and morality to be the chief motive of their aggression on revolutionary and republican France. Justice, as well as sincere respect for the memory of a most amiable woman, calls upon me to add that, to the best of my belief, the Princess, whose name is mixed up in this disgusting story, was entirely free from all reproach on that occasion. An education in such a court as Berlin was not likely to produce, and probably did not produce, any great austerity of principle; but the Duchess of York was certainly distinguished through life for the gentleness and frankness of her disposition, the soundness of her judgment, the constancy and generosity of her attachments to her family, her friends, and her dependents. Her understanding was far superior to the illusions which a station such as hers generally creates. She made, indeed, no ostentation of her philosophy, but she silently exerted it, not only in the regulation of her own conduct, but in softening and concealing both the political and private errors of those with whom she was connected. Had her husband lived to be king, the country, as well as he, would have seen fresh reasons for regretting her untimely end. As Duchess of York, her unobtrusive character concealed many of her good and shining qualities from the eye of the public. A disdain of popularity in high rank, combined with endowments to command it, has, at least, the merit of rarity and self-denial; and I trust it is a pardonable digression in these notes to bear testimony* to the virtues of one who from that motive, or from the still more laudable feelings of tenderness for others, forebore, during her lifetime, to draw upon the public for her due share of gratitude and applause.

To return: I have seen, but never was presented to her father, Frederick William II. However irregular in morals, he was not devoid of superstition. In 1792, he was much under the influence of a sect then famous in Germany, and called the *Illuminés*. Of that association of visionaries and impostors, his favorite, Mr. Bischoffswerder, was a member; and he is much belied if he did not resort to conjuration and apparitions, for the purpose of converting the King to his views of policy, which were very versatile and changeable, and not unfrequently as mysterious and unintelligible as his belief in necromacy, magic, and an immaterial world. Some odious and many ludicrous instances of the delusions practiced to engage the King in the war, and nearly as many of similar artifices to wean him from the prosecution of it, were circulated and credit-

* Lord Lauderdale was requested by the Duke of York to supply an epitaph for her monument. He applied to me, and I believe the lines I wrote are engraved on the tablet in Weybridge or Walton Church, erected to her memory.

ed throughout Europe. Many, no doubt, were invented; and most, in all likelihood, considerably heightened by public report; but there could hardly be so much exaggeration without some truth, and the notorious prevalence of such superstitions in all the courts of Germany rendered the stories probable enough, though I neither recollect the details, nor have examined the authorities on which they rested, sufficiently to justify my recording them as facts. Some years afterward it became a fashion or an artifice among the servile apologists of tyranny, to connect the sect of *Illuminés*, and all their ramifications, first with freemasonry, and afterward with the disorganizing and irreligious principles of the revolutionary clubs in France. I believe they were entirely distinct in their origin, their objects, and their progress. It is, at least, whimsical, that the only known practical result of such visionary practices on the events of the political world, was to prevail on many petty, and one important court of Germany, to inflict the calamities of war on mankind, for the purpose of rescuing the institutions of monarchy, popery, and nobility from destruction. If the more recent secret societies of Tugenbund in Germany, and Carbonari in Italy, really sprang out of them (a supposition in itself highly questionable), even those associations were formed in an anti-Gallican spirit, and contrived for the purpose of resisting the power of Napoleon, in the two quarters of Europe which became the theatres of their machinations.

In 1793 I visited Madrid, and my subsequent travels, as well as some accidental circumstances, have made me better acquainted with the events and characters connected with that court than with those of any other on the Continent.

Florida Blanca was not only dismissed and exiled, but so strictly confined in the citadel of Pampeluna, that I was not allowed to transmit a common letter of introduction to him from Lord Lansdown, when I passed through that town in 1793. He declined seeing me at Murcia in 1803, and after some correspondence with him on the revolution of 1808, at which period he became President of the Central Junta, I arrived too late to see him at Seville, where he died early in 1809. He had been originally promoted from the Embassy at Rome to be Prime Minister, by Charles III., probably at the recommendation of his predecessor; for it was a maxim of that methodical and tenacious Prince to give his ministers, on their dismissal, retirement, or death, the nomination of their successors. Florida Blanca or Moñino had the merits of his early profession, the law—application, accuracy, and perseverance in business. He improved some branches of the administration, and in foreign negotiations showed both zeal and spirit, combined with an adequate knowledge of the real interests of his country. He had, moreover, the dexterity to evade, and on occasions even to resist that formidable power the Church, without provoking its resentment or scandalizing its fanatical adherents. On the other hand, he was harsh, vindictive, and unjust, very jealous of his power, and mischievously active in extending ministerial authority at the expense and in defiance of the few remaining institutions of the state; all of which he endeavored to humiliate and corrupt. He strove to convert the grandees into mere appendages to the pageantry of the court, the magistrates into servile instruments of the minister of the day. He succeeded but too well. Charles

III. enjoined his son to continue him in office, and Charles IV. considered the injunction as sacred. It required time and intrigue to conquer his repugnance to any change. Perhaps his scruples would never have yielded, but for an accident which gave to the resolution the appearance, and indeed the reality of an act of justice arising out of virtuous indignation at misconduct. Florida Blanca had instigated a prosecution for a libel against a certain Marquis of Mancas, employed formerly as Spanish envoy at Copenhagen. In his eagerness to procure a sentence against him, he had the imprudence to dictate it in a letter to the President or acting President of the Council of Castile, whom he knew to be subservient to his designs. While the courier was on his way from the Escurial to Madrid, the President died of an apoplexy. The letter being directed to the title of office, not to the name of the individual, was delivered to and opened by the next in succession,* to whom the duty of presiding in the court had devolved. He happened to be either an upright magistrate, or a man devoted to the party already formed against the prime minister. He accordingly dispatched a copy of the letter to the King, who, justly incensed at so indecent an interference with the course of justice, and urged no doubt by the Queen, overcame all scruples of breaking his promise to his father, and first removed and then banished

* The story as here related was told me at Burgos in 1804, by Mancas, and has been confirmed to me by others. I had inserted it as a preliminary note to Florida Blanca's statement of his administration in MS., which I lent to Mr. Cox; and that complier printed my note, without asking my permission, together with the papers of the minister, in his History of the House of Bourbon, in Spain.

and imprisoned the premier. The motives of the Queen were not so pure as those professed by her party, and really acted upon by her husband, her amorous constitution had been well known to the old king. It could be no secret to his Minister. Charles III. used to smile at the simplicity of his son, who is said frequently to have remarked to him that princes were exempt from the lot to which too many husbands were exposed; first, because their wives were more strictly educated than private women; and, secondly, because, if viciously inclined, they could seldom find any royal personages with whom they could indulge such evil propensities. To such remarks the old man would suddenly but archly reply by bantering the prince* on his simplicity, or by muttering a favorite maxim of his own,† by no means complimentary to the chastity of the fair sex. Among the lovers of the Princess of the Asturias, whom Charles III. had from time to time removed from the court, was a young Garde du Corps of the name of Godoy, a native of Badajoz. His younger brother, Don Manuel, was in the same service, and undertook to convey the love letters of his exiled brother to his royal mistress. But her passion was not of a character to be long satisfied with expressions of tenderness from an absent lover. Don Manuel perhaps thought that he should promote the interests of his brother, as he unquestionably did his own, more effectually, by imitating his example than obeying his injunctions. In short, he supplanted him in the affections of his mistress, and at the accession of her husband to the throne was known at court to be her established lover. Count Florida Blanca had too much sagacity not to discover the

* Carlos, Carlos que tonto, que eres. † Todas, sí todas son putas.

character of the young favorite. He perceived, with much chagrin, that mere honors and distinctions would not satisfy him, that he aimed at a share at least of political power. But the old minister was too jealous to yield even to the obvious policy of admitting any partner in that concern. He had such plausible grounds in the extreme ignorance as well as inferior rank of his youthful candidate for office, that he could not but succeed for a time in excluding him from a seat in Council. The ruin, therefore, of Florida Blanca became necessary to the advancement of Godoy. Hence the eagerness of the Queen to accumulate charges against him, and to lay the catalogue of his offenses before the eyes of the King. She did not, however, venture to elevate Godoy at once to the highest situation in the state. The Marquis of Aranda, an Arragonese Grandee, was designated, by his reputation and the choice of the King, as the natural successor of an experienced prime minister. It was, however, suspected that he, on this occasion, stooped to purchase the nomination by promising to discover in the young Garde du Corps great aptitude for political affairs, and to recommend him to a high place in the councils of his sovereign. Under his auspices, Godoy was introduced into the cabinet. Aranda was in real character an Arragonese, stiff, unbending, and sarcastic; in politics a Frenchman, attached from habit and conviction to a strict alliance between the two countries; in principle a modern philosopher, well read in Voltaire, d'Alembert, and Helvetius; jealous of the Church, inveterate against the Jesuits, who had been suppressed during his first ministry, and not insensible to the somewhat exaggerated praises lavished upon him for that measure by those who had rendered infidelity fashionable in Paris, and afterward connected it in some degree with the cause of the French Revolution. In spite, therefore, of his attachment to the House of Bourbon and his intimacy with good company at Paris, he was less disposed to an anti-revolutionary confederacy than almost any European minister, and certainly than any in the service of a court connected by ties of blood with that of Versailles. Godoy, in quest of an opportunity for making his importance felt by differing with the premier, perceived that the instances of foreign powers, the increasing excesses of the French democracy, and the national as well as religious feelings of the Spaniards, would soon make war inevitable. He recommended it in council, and thus ingratiated himself with a powerful and increasing party. It is said that Aranda, heedless of consequences, and forgetful of the policy which had induced him to acquiesce in the young favorite's advancement, could not contain his surprise at his venturing to differ on such topics, and treated both the advice and adviser with utter scorn and contempt. If so, he very much miscalculated his strength. His pacific system, however reasonable, was easily overthrown. The fears of the great, and the fanaticism of the vulgar, applauded the new councilor for questioning its propriety. Friend and foe combined to render it impracticable. The execution of Louis XVI. seemed to justify and even to popularize a declaration of war, and English, German, and emigrant influence was exerted to procure the dismissal of Aranda. He was accordingly removed, or, as the Spanish phrase is, indulged or regaled* with his retirement. The

* Jubilado.

gentleness of his fall seemed to imply that Godoy, now Duke of Alcudia, was not altogether unmindful of his good offices, that he was more presumptuous and aspiring than vindictive or ungrateful in his nature. Aranda lost neither rank nor emolument by his dismissal; but he had impaired the dignity and lessened the weight of his character by this second short-lived administration, which in truth only paved the way for an obnoxious upstart and favorite.

Although I visited the lines at Yrun and St. Jean de Luz, I know little of the events of the war, and less of the Spanish generals who commanded. Ricardos* was reckoned an accomplished officer, the Count de la Union a young man of spirit and enterprise. General Caro, whom I did know, was a rough, bold veteran, whose notions of war were borrowed, I suspect, from the bull-fights, the theatre of the exploits of his youth. O'Reilly was once named General-in-chief, but died (some idly said of poison) in his way to the command. When a young Irish† adventurer, and ensign in the Spanish service, he saved his life in a battle in Italy, by persuading the dragoon who had struck him down, and was about to dispatch him, that he was the Duke of Arcos, the commander of the Spanish forces. He gained the favor of

* His family name was Richards; he was of English or Irish extraction, and in the line, if I am not mistaken, of a baronetcy.

† Any one conversant with the modern military history of Spain, or with good society in that country, must be struck with the large proportion of their eminent officers who were either born or descended from those who were born in Ireland. The comment which that circumstance furnishes upon our exclusive and intolerant laws, is obvious enough.

the court he served by rejecting, when prisoner, all the offers of Laudon to engage him in the Imperial service. His exploits at Algiers were not brilliant, and those in Louisiana were said to have done little credit to his humanity. As governor of Cadiz, he displayed great activity, vigor, and sagacity, and obtained a high reputation for political wisdom and courage. This and the favor of Charles III., who was wont to praise him for having, like a large elm which stood inconveniently in the middle of the road at Aranjuez, but which he would never allow to be felled, no friend but himself, procured for him twice the appointment of Prime Minister. In both instances the nomination was recalled, and another substituted, before he could arrive at Madrid. His death, on the way to the command of an army, seemed to complete the fatality attending the attainment of all his objects of ambition. He was quick, coarse, and shrewd ; thoroughly acquainted with the court and people with whom he had to deal, and of parts and courage to avail himself of his knowledge ; but he was not exempt from those failings in taste and judgment which are so often objected to his countrymen, and which not unfrequently mar the fortunes of men, otherwise best qualified to succeed in the race for power and distinction. The triumph of the Spaniards in Roussillon was short-lived. The French became the invaders in the beginning of 1794, and although the abhorrence of infidelity was in full force throughout Spain, and the adjoining province of Catalonia distinguished for anti-Gallican as well as military spirit, yet the French had great prospects of success from the jealousy subsisting between the Catalans and the regular forces, from the imperfect equipment and irregular pay of the troops, from the dearth of military talent in the Spanish officers, and from the propensity to intrigue and cabal in the councils of Charles IV. The danger grew manifest, and the war unpopular. The Catalans offered to defend their fortresses and frontiers at their own expense, but annexed two conditions: first, of naming their own officers; second, of the removal of all Castilian as well as emigrant troops from the principality. Such a hint that the means of defense were only to be purchased by a surrender of some portion of authority, was well calculated to check the martial ardor of an enervated court. It contributed to dispose the favorite to a peace with the Republic of France, now rendered a shade less obnoxious by the downfall of Robespierre, and the triumph of a party more equivocal in its principles, but less revolting and sanguinary in its conduct. The revolution in France of July, 1794, better known by the name of the 9th of Thermidor, and the softened tone of the succeeding governments, had, in the course of a year, together with the military triumphs of the revolutionary armies, reconciled or compelled some powers to sue for peace and court the alliance of the Republic. The Great Duke of Tuscany, at the suggestion of Manfredini (an enlightened pupil of the Emperor Joseph's school), who was his preceptor, favorite, and chamberlain, concluded a treaty with France in February, 1795. The King of Prussia followed that example before the summer was over. Spain had equal motives and greater means of appeasing the hostility of the fierce democracy. Her provinces were defenseless, but she had colonies and money wherewith to ransom them. That favorite French object—a strict union with Spain, or, to speak more correctly, a feverish dread of any permanent alliance between Spain and England—had devolved from the Bourbons to the Demagogues. One of the leaders who had signalized himself in the overthrow of Robespierre was likely, through the same propitious influence which had animated his exertions on that memorable occasion, to lend a favorable ear to any overture from Spain. The lady who bestowed her hand upon Tallien, as the incentive or reward of his glorious conduct on the 9th of Thermidor, and who, if she had some of the frailties, had all the generosity and gentleness, with a double portion of the beauty and grace which distinguished her countrywomen, was a Spaniard by birth. The noble use which she made of the influence which her exquisite beauty so naturally commanded, should have rescued her from that neglect in which the hypocrisy of the Consular and Imperial, and the ingratitude of the Bourbon governments have left her for years. She was the daughter of Cabarrus, a French merchant, whose adventurous spirit and talents procured him some of the honors and more of the vicissitudes of a statesman in Spain. He had planned and founded the Bank of San Carlos, connected himself with many leading characters in the country, and was banished and confined on the suppression or failure of that establishment. He was subsequently removed to Madrid, where he was still under arrest when, at the instance of the Countess of Galvez, the Duke of Alcudia employed him to convey an overture to the Republic by means of the correspondence which subsisted between him and his daughter, Madame Tallien. He acquitted himself so well of that and subsequent commissions, that the Spanish Ministry admitted his contested claims on the State, and liquidated them to the amount of 6,000,000 of reals. He was no doubt consulted on the terms of the peace, and his daughter contributed to the completion of the treaty (a work well suited to her gentle mind), which was signed, to the surprise of the Austrian and English Governments, on the 22d of July, 1795, at Basle in Switzerland. Popular applauses and court honors lavished on Godoy for this treaty made ample amends for the remonstrances of the allies with which he was harassed, and the invectives of the English press by which he was assailed. He was created Prince of the Peace. The vocabulary of titles was exhausted to express the favor of the court, and privileges of a new and ludicrous nature were invented to mark the sense entertained by his Sovereign of his wisdom and success. As a specimen may be selected, the right of bearing an image of Janus before him on all solemn occasions—an emblem, says the patent, of his knowledge and foresight, which, like that false divinity, reflects on the past by regarding what is behind him; and provides for the future by surveying equally all that is before him. He seemed, however, at that time desirous of deserving the unparalleled honors he had attained, for he endeavored to confer some benefits on the community from which he derived them. At least his administration, from the conclusion of the treaty of Basle to the temporary decline of his favor in 1798, showed, notwithstanding the bad policy and worse conduct of a war with England, more disposition to reform abuses and to improve the condition of the people of Spain, and, above all, to reward, encourage, and promote every kind of useful talent, than is discernible in any other epoch of his long possession of power. Possibly, some occurrences at court reminded him that his tenure of authority was precarious, and that his mistress was neither from his example nor her own nature likely to prove a model of fidelity. Such apprehensions might induce him to court popularity, to gain partisans, and to build his power, if possible, on more honorable and solid foundations. Symptoms of jealousy were remarked at a very early period; but the Queen had taken such pains to ingratiate her lover with the King, that she then and at many subsequent periods found it difficult to impair, much more to destroy, the work of her own contrivance. Through their mysterious connection, the ascendency of Godoy over the mind of the King seemed as strong as that he had assumed over his mistress. Yet his amours, which exasperated the latter as infidelities, might, he well knew, be employed to shake the confidence of Charles, who had been taught to revere the austerity of his morals as much as to admire the extent of his capacity. It has, indeed, been asserted that his marriage with the daughter of the Infant Don Louis originated in a malicious trait of jealousy of the Queen. The story goes, that she brought the King unexpectedly to the apartment of the favorite, and surprised him when supping *tête-à-tête* with Mademoiselle Tudo, a lady of extraordinary beauty* to whom he was clandestinely married, though some say by

* She was daughter of an artillery officer of some merit, and had come with her mother, a widow, to solicit a pension at St. Ildefonso, where she was introduced by the Baylio Valdez, Minister of Marine, to the Duke of Alcudia.

a contract which the laws would consider as invalid; that the King was partly shocked and partly diverted at the discovery; that he shortly afterward, at the suggestion of the Queen, with a view of providing, without the peril of a deadly sin, for the incontinence of his favorite, insisted on matrimony, and condescended to offer his young and recently acknowledged cousin for a bride; that the Prince of the Peace, not daring to acknowledge his union with the Tudo, and still less to decline the royal alliance without alleging some such insurmountable bar, prevailed on the wife of his affections to suppress the truth, and allowed Charles, in his zeal to rescue him from more venial and ordinary vices, to involve him in the heinous and troublesome sin of bigamy. I do not vouch for the truth of the tale. Well-informed persons believed it, and related it to me. It is certain that the ostensible marriage with the Princess, which took place in 1797, never interrupted his connection with the Tudo. During his prosperity, she was generally lodged in a royal palace or in an adjoining apartment. After his exile and adversity, she followed him to Rome, and has been always treated by him, his friends, and even the Royal Family, as a personage in some sort legitimately entitled to the society, tenderness, and protection of the Prince of the Peace. His more splendid alliance did not render him more secure of the countenance of favor at court, or less disposed to seek for such assistance as talents in office, and an enlightened government could bestow. He consulted M. Cabarrus on the formation of a new Ministry nearly at the epoch of his nuptials, and that judicious and well-informed friend recommended the Spaniards best qualified to discharge the trust with credit to his choice and benefit to the country. Such were Don Francisco Saavedra, and Don Gaspar Melchor de Jovellanos. The first, with whom I was afterward slightly acquainted at Seville,* had filled high offices in the colonies, and enjoyed at home and abroad great reputation for abilities and integrity. The French always took a particular interest in his fate, though his principles led him to concur in the national resistance to the government which Napoleon endeavored in 1808 to impose upon Spain.

Jovellanos, whom I knew more intimately, and respected most sincerely, was an Asturian of good family, educated at the Colegios Mayores, patronized, if I mistake not, by his countryman Campomanes, and distinguished at an early period of life for his literary productions in verse and prose, his taste in the arts, his proficiency in the law, and his extensive knowledge in all branches of political economy. Great as were his intellectual endowments, his moral qualities were in unison with them. The purity of his taste was of a piece with that of his mind, and the correctness of his language a picture of his well-regulated life. In the persuasive smoothness of his eloquence, and the mild dignity of his demeanor, one seemed to read the serenity of his temper, and the elevation of his character. *Erant mores qualis facundia.* He had filled offices in the magistracy, and sometimes as a reward, sometimes as a

* In 1810. When in 1803, I asked General Beurnonville at Madrid to use his interest in mitigating the imprisonment of Jovellanos, he told me that he had instructions from his court to exert all he had in favor of Saavedra, in the first instance; and that until he was liberated, he did not conceive himself authorized in making any application for his fellow-sufferer.

contrivance for removing him, the superintendence of public institutions in the provinces had been confided to his care. He discharged these various duties with great zeal and intelligence, and had in all given general satisfaction; for the complacency with which he contemplated the success of a member of his family, a student of his college, or a native of his province, never degenerated into partiality. It was a proof of the amiable affections of his nature, which disposed him to rejoice at the merit and reward of such as he was directly or remotely connected with. If such feelings ever biased his choice of a public servant, interest certainly never had that effect. He offended the Queen by his uncourtly austerity on such points. His refusal to promote her creatures passed with her for intolerable rudeness; and when he asked in what school some ignorant man whom she recommended for the magistracy, had acquired the elements of his profession, she tartly answered, "In the same college where you studied politeness." The sarcasm was unmerited. None could reproach Jovellanos with want of urbanity or courtesy but such as exacted under those names an obsequiousness in manner and a subserviency in action to which no honorable nature will submit. He has been somewhat more plausibly accused of overstrained scruples and ill-timed remonstrances on the licentious conduct of the Prince of the Peace. He has even been taxed with ingratitude, for not protecting from the displeasure of the court a man to whose interference he, in some measure, owed his elevation in it. He no doubt saw the influence of the favorite decline with some indifference. Perhaps he was more observant of the private vices which lowered the character of his government, than mindful of that capricious exertion of public virtue which had raised him and Saavedra to a seat in it. But he was never suspected of accelerating what was then considered as the fall of the favorite, nor did it depend on him to prevent it. He did not sacrifice his place, or his hopes of doing his country some service, to one to whom he had some obligations, but for whom he could not feel much respect. Such is the sum and front of his offending, even if the facts alleged, which are disputable, were granted. It was natural for the Prince of the Peace to resent his neglect, but the offense, consisting entirely of omissions, was surely not of a magnitude to justify, to palliate, or even to account for, the persecutions to which Jovellanos was exposed on the return of the Prince to power. As it must be acknowledged that the Prince was seldom guilty of any act approaching to cruelty, I am inclined to attribute the imprisonment of Jovellanos in Majorca, and the contumely and insult to which he was there subjected, chiefly to the Queen. Saavedra told his friend, when they were once more united in the councils of their country at Seville, in 1809, that the Queen was unaccountably persuaded that he (Jovellanos) was the author or the patron of an obscene libel printed at Paris and quite unknown to him which was entitled *Les trois Reines*, and contained a slanderous description of the private and political vices of the Queens of France, Naples, and Spain. She hardly concealed her aversion to him, even while he was Minister. In truth, the purity of his private life was not likely to reconcile her to the inflexibility of his public principles. He was, if not in creed, in character and political austerity, a Jansenist, and connected with many of that sect, who, in Spain, as in other Roman Catholic countries, have always been found the least corruptible and most consistent party in the state. What were the causes of that estrangement between the Prince of the Peace and the Queen may not be easy to ascertain. The effects became obvious early in 1798. There were good grounds for jealousy on both sides. The Prince, after his marriage with the Princess, still remained attached to *the Tudo*, as the wife of his choice was called; and the Queen, before his separation from the court, had become enamored of an officer of the name of *Mallo*, whose gallantry, to use the most delicate term, had nothing moral or intellectual to recommend it. She is said to have lavished sums of money on her new favorite. A story was current at Madrid which, if true, would at once prove that the Prince of the Peace was aware of her infidelities to him, and disposed to revenge himself in a way no woman could easily submit to or forgive. The King, the Queen, and the Prince of the Peace, said this tale, were at a window in the palace of Aranjuez, when Mallo drove by in his curricle. Charles IV. expressed some surprise at a young officer of low rank and narrow fortune possessing so brilliant an equipage; on which the Prince assured his Majesty that it was easily, though somewhat ludicrously, to be accounted for. "An old, rich, and toothless woman" (for he knew the Queen had a set of teeth from Paris) "had fallen madly in love with that *Mallo*, and she furnished him with many equipages, horses, and every luxury in which he had a mind to indulge." Charles laughed immoderately at the storv, and whenever the name of the gallant occurred, was eager to circulate the amusing piece of scandal, which diverted him exceedingly, but he little knew or suspected concerned him and his so nearly. The anecdote is, perhaps, too dramatic to deserve implicit credit. It was believed by many well-informed persons, and I repeat it as I received it. Whether from resentment, jealousy, or fear, the Queen was supposed at that period to labor hard to dispel the charm she had been at such pains to form, and to infuse into the mind of the King distrust of the man whom she had recommended so successfully to his confidence, and who was now allied by marriage to the Royal Family. She so far prevailed that Charles IV. disparaged in conversation those talents and services he had formerly prized so highly and extolled so extravagantly. He is represented as having once expressed a wish that some one would throw the favorite out of the window, and rid him of so troublesome a connection. He did indeed in fact, though not in form, forbid his appearance at the Sitios, except upon special permission or invitation. Yet when the harsh measures usual on a change of ministry in Spain are considered and compared with the treatment experienced by the Prince of the Peace on this occasion, it must be acknowledged that some mysterious link of love or fear seems, even during an ostensible separation of the parties, to have subsisted between him and the court.*

In the meanwhile the Queen was more capricious and licentious in her conduct. Urquijo who, on the rupture with England in 1796, had returned from that country and become, in virtue of his rank in the public office, chief

* See Appendix, No. II.

clerk, acted as secretary during the illness of his principal, Don Francisco Saavedra. That minister continued ill for some time, and it was necessary that some one conversant with the routine of office should, according to usage, read the dispatches to their Majesties. To give Urquijo the requisite rank for such an honor, he was nominally appointed embassador to the Batavian Republic, and attended standing before a table at which the King and Queen were seated to read the official correspondence. Urquijo was young, handsome, and well made. Her Majesty was more struck by the reader than edified by the dispatches. In defiance of etiquette, if not of propriety, she bade him take a chair and read the papers at his ease. Such condescension was the forerunner of greater favors. He was soon Minister of Foreign Affairs. Saavedra and Jovellanos were removed and banished; but as the removal of both, especially of Saavedra, was preceded by illness, many who hated the Queen, and some who hated the Prince of the Peace, ascribed their maladies to poison, administered, according to the version of the former, with a view of facilitating the promotion of Urquijo, and, according to the equally improbable surmises of the latter, to revenge the ingratitude and elude the enmity of those two ministers toward the discarded favorite. Stories of poison are easily invented and readily believed; but not only the atrocity of the crime, but the difficulty of the perpetration, especially in the cases of persons surrounded with pomp and ceremony, should dispel all suspicion of such guilt, unless it be substantiated by testimony, and corroborated by undeniable circumstances. The Queen of Spain could ruin a minister without such difficult practices. If the Prince had any prospect of resuming his favor at court, he knew that court too well to apprehend that the remonstrances of grave and austere ministers would be any bar to his resumption of power. Whatever, therefore, might be the animosity either of the Queen or Prince against those two ministers, they had prospects of gratifying it without resorting to so heinous, and, above all, so dangerous yet so uncertain a crime.* I am satisfied, therefore, that the rumor was groundless in the instance of these ministers; and I am equally inclined to disbelieve many other tales of similar practices of the Queen. I must, however, acknowledge that a Sicilian of the name of Carappa, suspected, in 1804, of gallantries with the Princess of Asturias, was himself persuaded that his health had been impaired at that time by potions administered to him by the contrivances of the Queen of Spain. He adduced what he called his proofs to me at Rome, ten years afterward, but they were not convincing to my mind, though I believe they were so to his. The administration of Urquijo, with whom I was never personally acquainted, lasted longer than, according to the strange stories reported of him, could have appeared probable to any reasonable man. He was ignorant, rash, and presumptuous in the extreme. Averse to every institution of the country and every opinion of the people he was called upon to govern, he determined, nevertheless, to slight the individuals, as well as to overlook the precautions, most necessary to the execution of his arduous undertakings. So fanatically hostile was he to the Church of

* Those who believe in the story must acknowledge the difficulty and uncertainty of an attempt to poison any one, inasmuch as neither Saavedra nor Jovellanos died.

Rome, that when, being chargé d'affaires in London, he first heard that General Bonaparte, by the peace of Tolentino, and at the intervention of the Spanish embassador Azara, had spared the Papal government, he ran like a maniac from his house for more than a mile on the Uxbridge road, and threw himself in despair into a pond. Mr. Carlisle* the surgeon, who told me the story, happened to pass by when he was dragged out in a state of insensibility, and superintended his recovery by the means recommended by the Humane Society. When our Secretary of State called on him, he made a point of receiving him with Paine's Age of Reason, magnificently bound, on the table; and Lord Grenville has more than once accounted to me for the low opinion he entertains of Spanish politicians, by the circumstance of Urquijo, the wildest and most incapable man he ever transacted business with, being elevated to the station of First Minister. Recommended to the Queen by his personal beauty alone, he is said to have slighted her advances, and throughout his administration, to have preferred, even to ostentation, the Princess Branciaforte, sister of the Prince of the Peace, his most dangerous rival. Intent on various reforms—such as the suppression of the Inquisition and of several monastic institutions, the appointment of a patriarch, and the transferrence of all Spanish causes from the Dataria at

* This is a strange, almost an incredible story, but I give my authority. I made Mr. Carlisle repeat it to me above once, and he mentioned many circumstances attending the event, and assured me that he had maintained an intimacy and correspondence with Urquijo ever after. I met Mr. Carlisle at the house of Mr. P. Knight, in Soho-square.

Rome to national tribunals—he began by removing from office and from court those men whose talents, gravity, and principles, by shedding some lustre on his measures, might have softened the odium to which such daring innovations must obviously have been exposed. He seemed to look for support from the foreign ministers exclusively. He was much connected with Valcknaer, the minister from the Batavian Republic, and Borel, the Saxon envoy. At the instance of the latter, he engaged in a negotiation to effect a marriage between the Prince of Asturias and a princess of Saxony, with whom he expected a considerable dowry. The King and Queen were brought to acquiesce in the design, but the old Elector had scruples in sending his daughter to so immoral a court. He was reconciled to the measure by the notable expedient of marrying his sister, a woman of fifty, to the King of Spain's brother, the Infant Don Antonio, who had never hitherto been allowed the solace of a wife, or indeed any other, but that of cooking and eating his own dinner, and killing some half tame rabbits for it, in a small island of the Tagus, in Aranjuez, set apart for his princely diversion, inasmuch as both his father and his elder brother had always been too selfish to let him partake of their sport. The scheme of the Saxon marriages, if it did not contribute in some degree to the downfall of Urquijo, shared the fate of that minister. It was abandoned on his disgrace, and the Saxon minister, after being unjustly accused of purloining minerals from the Museum, and exposed to many other unmanly and ungenerous persecutions, went mad, and died of vexation and chagrin. Urquijo, from self-sufficiency, was always confident of his own favor at court, and of the weakness of his adversaries, especially the Prince of the Peace. Though warned even by his sister of the imprudence of such a step, he allowed him to re-appear at the Sitios. A cabal was formed between the formidable favorite, the Nuncio, and the dignified clergy who dreaded the design of appointing a patriarch and withdrawing all submission to the Dataria at Rome. They alarmed Charles IV. with the prospect of a schism in the church; and it is said that a remonstrance against the plans of the reforming minister, and a labored statement of the consequences to be apprehended, were presented by the Nuncio to the King himself at St. Ildefonso, when Urquijo had proceeded to Madrid. Whether the Queen was a party to this intrigue or not, I do not know. From returning love for the Prince, or from fear, she acquiesced; for it is certain that Urquijo was dismissed, banished, and imprisoned in the citadel of Pampeluna in 1800, and that from that period the Prince of the Peace, who recommended his cousin Don Pedro Cevallos to the Foreign Office, and was himself ever after recognized in the privacy of the Royal Family by the endearing name of Manuelito, recovered all his pristine power. He seemed less desirous to exert it in a manner creditable to himself and useful to the country. He had been recently indebted to the clergy, and was more subservient to the court and Church of Rome than his principles or temper had formerly led him to be. His resentment at what he considered to be the ingratitude of Jovellanos, estranged him from persons enlightened by literature and philosophy, as well as from that austere party or sect in Spain who may be designated as Jansenists. Jovellanos was torn from his retreat at Gijon, and immured in the dungeons or convents of Majorca, with the contumelious addition to the sentence itself (pronounced without trial, and even charge), that he should study his catechism under the superintendence of the ignorant inmates of a monastery. Persons obnoxious to the favorite or to the Queen were denounced to the Inquisition as Jansenists, and exposed to all the terrific forms and proceedings of that merciless establishment. It must be acknowledged, that in the instance of two brothers of the name of La Cuesta, canons, I think, of Palencia, that odious but independent tribunal disdained to become the servile instrument of ministerial injustice, and manfully acquitted, released, and indemnified the prisonors. Truth is, the Prince of the Peace was never in his heart a friend of the Church of Rome, nor a patron of the Inquisition. Still less was he a partisan of the French, though his cowardice and vanity occasionally rendered him subservient to their designs. It was no doubt at their instigation that he made war upon Portugal. So elated was he at the petty conquest of Olivenza, that he not only indulged his ostentation by sending a branch of orange to the Queen, but with ludicrous self-complacency compared himself publicly to the great King of Prussia, accepted the extravagant compliments of the French as sincere marks of admiration, and verily persuaded himself, for some time, that his military character rendered Spain formidable to France and to the Chief Consul. His conduct with respect to his allies, from the Portuguese campaign, and still more from the peace of Amiens, was a medley of inconsistency, presumption, temerity, perfidy, and irresolution almost unequaled in history. He at one time assumed a tone of menace and hostility, which in the circumstances of the two countries was quite preposterous; insisting on some impracticable or unreasonable concession, and instructing the embassador to declare war against the Republic or Empire; at others, he connived, I much fear with the approbation of English agents, at the introduction of assassins, the accomplices of Georges, into France; and sometimes he truckled to the most exorbitant pretensions of the French Government, and solicited from their power and partiality some unreasonable personal favor for himself. He had hardly embroiled his country in a second war with England, by an unseasonable compliance with the humor rather than the policy of Napoleon, before he wantonly affronted that great prince by a public proclamation, and yet more sensibly offended him by a proposal of a confederacy against France with a Northern Power. The French detected that design, in a correspondence which they found at Berlin, soon after their armies had taken possession of it, though Napoleon, very unaccountably, never assigned that fact in public or in private as an exculpation of his subsequent aggressions on Spain.

In the meanwhile the attention of the Prince of the Peace was absorbed by occupations more congenial to his taste and perhaps better suited to his talents, viz., the squabbles, jealousies, and intrigues of the Palace. He soon perceived that the Prince of Asturias, however inexperienced and apparently insensible, entertained a strong aversion and suspicion of him. He probably conjectured, perhaps he ascertained, that such hostile feelings were fomented by secret and occasional communications with the grandees. Some of that class plumed themselves on marking a distinction, immense in their estimation, between newly acquired and ancient hereditary honors, although their own titles were in all likelihood originally derived from sources as impure; they studiously conferred on the Prince of the Peace, in all intercourse by letter or conversation, these ceremonious terms of respect to which a Grandee is entitled from all, and generally receives from an inferior, but they carefully abstained from all those of familiarity and fellowship which is the usage, though not the legal etiquette, in Spain for persons equal in quality to exchange between one another. He was with them *Señor Duque, Señor Principe, Ussencia* or *Alteza;* and never "*tú,*" or any other word implying intimacy and equality. Among these the most distinguished was the Duke of Infantado. He had the advantages of youth, birth, a princely fortune, a good education, and an agreeable address. His pursuits were rational and manly; he had some ambition, and till called upon to take an active part in affairs, was thought to possess great capacity for them, combined with principles that would direct it to the benefit of his country. Perhaps it was unfortunate for the formation of his political character, that he was initiated in business of importance by a confidential intercourse with Ferdinand. The false, cowardly, and vindictive disposition of that prince was calculated to render all who dealt with him suspicious and irresolute ever afterward. At the period of his marriage in 1802, there was nothing but a sinister countenance in the Prince of Asturias to announce those odious qualities which have caused so much misery to his subjects. He showed little inclination to study, and still less to sports or amusements.

He seldom marked the slightest preference or affection to such as were admitted to his company. Some little aptitude to mathematics was observed in him, and he was said to take interest in the scientific part of fortification; but it was generally believed that he was weak both in character and intellect, and such a persuasion was encouraged at court. I have been, indeed, assured that even before his marriage, and during an illness of Charles IV. at St. Ildefonso, a plot was matured for setting him aside, or at least postponing his succession, on the score of incapacity, in case of the death of his father. According to the same information, Ferdinand had intimation of the design, and found means to convey it to the French Government, and the Chief Consul was on the point of interfering in his behalf, when the recovery of the King disconcerted the projects of both parties for a time. This circumstance was related to me more than twenty years afterward, and I think my informant must have mistaken the date, or confounded the occurrences of that day with many subsequent events.

For some months after the marriage, which was celebrated at Barcelona in 1802, it was apprehended that no issue could be expected. The Queen of Naples upbraided her embassador, the Duke of St. Theodore (from whom I derive my information), for having delivered over her favorite daughter to a joyless and barren bed. That minister, however, adroitly ascertained that ignorance and innocence, and no natural defect or coldness of constitution, had retarded the completion of their union. He found means ere long of enlightening the royal pupils, and even of satisfying his more experienced mistress that he had not been unsuccessful in his instructions. The details related to me would make a figure in a modern Brantôme, but I do not aspire to be such, and I leave them to the imaginations of Jews or Christians, who may read these pages, with an assurance that their fancy can hardly make them more ludicrous or indelicate than reality. The bride was a pale, sickly, ugly young woman, with a gentle expression of countenance and great propriety of manner. She soon lost, or never possessed the affections of her mother-in-law. Soon after her pregnacy was announced, a miscarriage ensued; and it was ascribed by common report to ill-usage or yet more criminal practices of the Queen. It was not long ere the court suspected or affected to suspect the young Princess of gallantry. She was more than once confined to her apartment by an order from the King. Importance and mystery were attached to the arrest and dismissal of a young Sicilian in the Garde du Corps, of the name of Carappa. To his story and illness I have before alluded. I think it was at the same time hinted to the Duchess of St. Theodore that her presence at Madrid would for some time be dispensed with. Pains were certainly taken to imply that both an amour, and a political intrigue to give the Neapolitans an ascendency in the court of the heir-apparent, had been detected or defeated. It was much believed at this period (1804), that the Council of Castile had been consulted on the practicability and propriety of setting Ferdinand aside, and that it had answered, "that there was no known authority which could deprive of his right of succession a Prince of Asturias duly *sworn*, *married*, and *honored*."* If such a proceeding

* Jurado, casado, y honrado.

actually took place, which I never could ascertain,* the answer was more in unison with the ancient maxims of Castile and Arragon, than suited to the ears of a Prince of the House of Bourbon. It derived the right to the Crown from an oath administered in Cortes, or in deputations thereof, and confined the enjoyment even of that right to such as were "*married*" and subsequently "*honored*" in the country; thereby implying an authority vested somewhere to divest even a sworn Prince who was either unmarried, or not respected in the nation, of his right of succession.

The Princess of Asturias did not long survive these discussions and reports. Public hatred of the Queen and of the favorite attributed her death without scruple, but also without proof or even inquiry, to poison. She had always the appearance of bad health, and died no doubt a natural death. The period of it might, indeed, be accelerated by ill-treatment, vexation, and chagrin. The dissensions at court were not buried with her. On the contrary, the enmity between the Prince of Asturias and the favorite became more virulent, or at least more notorious. Ferdinand communicated his grievances first to his former preceptor Escoiquiz, and then through him to various Spaniards and some foreigners. At their suggestion, or from his own reflections, he conceived the project of concerting with the French Embassy the means of ruining the

* When I say I could never ascertain *it*, I mean the details and form of the proceeding; but of transactions and practices having an equivalent object in view, I have heard and seen many proofs, and among them a justificatory memoir of Caballero, then Minister of Grace and Justice, which distinctly showed that he was tampered with, though without effect, to concur in a design for setting aside the Prince of Asturias.

Prince of the Peace, and placing himself or his creatures at the head of the Spanish councils, and he added a proposal of allying himself by marriage with the House of Bonaparte,* an expedient to which he more than once reverted in the course of his life. Napoleon, whatever were his ultimate plans, was not averse to maintaining such a correspondence with the heir-apparent. He knew well that the predilections of the Prince of the Peace leaned to England rather than France. His ill-will had been manifested in public, and his more secret manœuvres had not escaped the vigilance of the French diplomacy. Beauharnais probably obeyed the spirit, though he may have exceeded the letter of his instructions, in encouraging the cabals of the Prince of Asturias and the Duke of Infantado, and in his subsequent communications with that party. He was certainly closely connected with them, and Murat afterward suspected him of sacrificing the interests of his country, and betraying the secrets of his court, from corrupt motives, to the adherents of Ferdinand; but it is pos-

* Stanislaus Girardin, a man of veracity and intimate with Joseph while King of Spain, assured me that Ferdinand wrote with his own hand to Napoleon or Joseph to congratulate them on the victory of Tudela !!! and at the same time repeated his solicitation for a matrimonial alliance with the House of Bonaparte. Many of the imperial councilors were for printing the letter in the *Moniteur*, with the hope of disgusting the enthusiastic partisans of Ferdinand with the baseness of their chief, but the Emperor observed not only that the knowledge of the transaction might hereafter be inconvenient, but the immediate object of the publication would be defeated by the very baseness which they hoped to expose. It was so bad that it would be disbelieved, and imputed as a forgery to him, the Emperor. He suppressed it.

sible and probable that Napoleon concealed from Murat much of the secret transactions and negotiations in Spain, when it suited his views to alter the course that had been pursued by his embassador. It is an undeniable fact that the party of Ferdinand was founded on an intimate alliance with France, and that all such interest in the Spanish councils as could be termed with any plausibility "English" depended entirely on the Prince of the Peace. That favorite had not, unfortunately, the spirit to avow, or the steadiness to execute, the system of policy he would have liked to pursue, even after he had detected the existence of the cabals and correspondence between the French agents and the Prince of Asturias. Ferdinand was, however, arrested. A guard was placed at his door in the Escurial, and his papers, portfolios, and furniture seized and conveyed to the King's apartment. His first step was to write a submissive letter to his mother. She answered that as he had suspected her as well as his father's ministers of designs against his interests and even his person, and as such suspicion was the cause or pretext of any improper proceedings in which he might be involved, delicacy and honor precluded her from interfering while the matter was under examination. She had determined to ask no question, and to deliver no opinion till the King was in full possession of all the evidence of which he was in search, and had formed an unbiased judgment on its nature and tendency. That then, if his anger continued, she might intercede to appease it, or at least to rescue her child from its consequences, but that she would not expose herself to misinterpretations by advice to either party, or by any comment on the causes or extent of his estrangement from her and his father's government. After two or three days' confinement, during which no intercourse was allowed, Ferdinand was brought before his father and mother. The seals which, if I mistake not, he had placed on his portfolios and boxes when they were taken from him, were broken in his presence. The papers found therein were read before him to the King. He once or twice in the course of the perusal of them entreated the Queen by looks or words to interpose; but she told him that she had wished to withdraw, and now repeated her application to Charles IV., who insisted on her remaining, and bade his son, with much passion, listen without interruption to what was read, and to what would afterward be alleged against him, and give him such answers and explanations as consistently with truth he was enabled to do. The whole contents of the papers have never, I believe, been divulged. Many were insignificant; some mere matters of form; others somewhat suspicious and unintelligible, but among them was the draft of a letter to Napoleon, soliciting a Princess of his Imperial House in marriage; and another of a very equivocal nature which both the Queen and the Duke of Infantado have described to me as written I think, and signed I am sure, in Ferdinand's own handwriting, *Yo El Rey.* It appointed some person (whose name did not appear in that draft or copy) Captain-General of Castile, and commanded him to arrest and imprison without delay the Prince of the Peace. The paper was long, probably in due form, and certainly containing the enumeration of titles and offices of the persons named therein, according to the usage of Spanish official documents. Charles IV. asked Ferdinand, with some vehemence, how he dared to draw such a paper, and annex such a signature? He said his head might answer it. It amounted to treason in law, and to parricide in intention. He threatened him, with much vociferation, with all the consequences, unless he instantly discovered at whose instigation he had taken so dangerous a step. Ferdinand, with more surprise than dismay, assured his father that he was laboring under a mistake, and converting a very harmless, though perhaps indecorous amusement, into a matter of state, swelling a childish impropriety into an act of premeditated guilt. The paper, he said, was a *jeu d'esprit* written for his diversion one evening in the Christmas holidays, with his late wife, and intended for a parody of official instruments, or at worst, a specimen of the power they should possess when it pleased Providence to deprive them of their father, the King of Spain. The Queen, who at Rome, in 1814, described this curious scene to me in the presence of her husband, assured me that Ferdinand gave this account so readily, and so naturally, that without acquitting him in her own mind of many other offenses, she was yet satisfied, as he told the story, that the paper formed no part of the conspiracy of which they were seeking the clew, but was, in truth, some childishness (*quelque enfantillage*) of her son and the late Princess of Asturias. But the King, more attentive than she to matters of rank, precedence, and promotion, quickly perceived that Godoy was designated by a title * conferred

* I think it was High Admiral or some such title. But I, like the Queen of Spain, am somewhat inobservant of matters of that sort, and am afraid of discrediting the substance of my narrative by trusting to my inaccurate memory as to form and detail.

upon him since the death of that Princess. Half choking with rage and clenching his fist, Charles exclaimed: "Tú mientes, Fernando, tú mientes; y tú me lo pagarás, sí, me lo pagarás." His fury alarmed the Queen, and might well terrify the Prince. But then ensued a scene which the Queen most truly characterized as the climax of baseness, cowardice, and perfidy. Ferdinand fell on his knees, burst into tears, acknowledged the charge, but, with strong promises of amendment, exculpated himself by casting the blame on all those with whom he had at any time conversed on such subjects. He exaggerated their hatred of the Prince of the Peace, described their designs as going far beyond his own, and spontaneously denounced the names of every one of them, offering every document in his power, and even his oral testimony, to convict them of the guilt in which, for his sake, they had involved themselves. The Queen assured me that she shuddered at the unfeeling baseness of his disclosures; she added, that the King was too much absorbed in his rage at the conspiracy, and too much bent on the punishment of the offenders, to view in its true light the treachery of his son, more disgusting if possible than any plot of which he could be suspected. Such was the account I received in 1814 from the Queen herself at Rome in the palace Barbarini. The King, who was present and attentive to her narrative, confirmed the greater part by his gestures, and acquiesced in the rest by his silence. It is corroborated by the proceedings which ensued. At the same time I should observe that the object of her Majesty's conversation with me was to justify her indignation against her son. Her narrative consequently ended here. The subsequent events I derive from less direct, but yet credible sources, and in many particulars from the Duke of Infantado. An order was dispatched to Madrid to convey that Duke, on the very night of this confession, to the Escurial; and there a commission was appointed to try him for high treason. He probably would have been executed immediately had he been brought thither according to orders; but the muleteers purposely missed the turn to the Escurial, and conveyed him as far as St. Ildefonso, before they acknowledged their pretended mistake. They had, it is supposed, been bribed by agents of the French Embassy to do so. In the mean while, Beauharnais bestirred himself to soften the anger of the King, to awaken the fears of the favorite, and, if he could not procure the liberation of Infantado and nis associates, to save them from the fatal consequences of a criminal proceeding instituted in the moment of resentment. Infantado, after some weeks' close confinement, was banished to Ecija. Ferdinand had on his first arrest contrived to apprise him; and he had prudently concealed the original paper signed *Yo El Rey*, and conferring on him the appointment of Captain-General of Castile, in a tin box which was buried in his mother's garden at Chamartin, and remained there when that villa became, in 1809, the head-quarters of Napoleon.* A proclamation was issued, stating the existence of a conspiracy, and the fiscal was employed to draw up an accusation against the conspirators; but the non-appearance of the original paper, which was searched for in vain, and the scandal, rather than the

* Napoleon placed his chair on the very spot on the morning before he entered Madrid, and spread the maps and plans before him in the garden.

reluctance of Ferdinand, the heir apparent, exhibiting himself in the characters of accomplice, informer, and witness, probably deterred the court from any further proceeding against the prisoners; for the circumstance on which in conversation the Duke of Infantado rested his main defense of the paper, would not, I presume, have been considered as conclusive evidence of his innocence. It was sealed with black wax, said the Duke, to prevent any use being made thereof till Charles IV. was actually dead. Thus the truth (added he) would have been inferred by any reasonable man, and it would have appeared, as it was, a mere measure of precaution to take effect, in case any thing should happen to his father, for the purpose of securing the successor to the Crown from intimidation from those in possession of the palace. It was a device by which any act forced upon him, and merely colored with his name, would have been annulled in the eyes of the public.

From this period, notwithstanding outward appearances of reconciliation between all the members of the Royal Family, and notwithstanding the subsistence of treaties, and a constant intercourse between France and Spain, the palace was a scene of cabal, enmity, and conspiracy, and the two *allied* governments in a state of ill-disguised distrust and hostility. Ferdinand looked to Napoleon and to French agents and *armies* exclusively for protection against the favorite, while the favorite wavered between the policy of defying, eluding, or propitiating the power of France. Another party was in the mean while formed among Spaniards of enlightened views, of which O'Farril and Asanza were in some sense the leaders. They intended to avail themselves of the approaching crisis to overturn, together with the power of Godoy, the tyranny both in Church and State; and they hoped through the ascendency of the Prince of the Asturias, and the revival or establishment of institutions really national, to provide against all future abuses, and to raise Spain in the scale of European States. Some of these persons had, indeed, strong predilections for France, and persuaded themselves that Napoleon would favor their designs, and even assist in laying the foundations of Spanish prosperity in the principles of a free government, as long as they continued to direct the resources resulting therefrom to the furtherance of his own projects against England. Napoleon, however, clearly perceived (whatever were his ulterior objects), that to secure his own interests upon the triumph of any party, or on the downfall of all, the presence of a French force was indispensable. He adroitly availed himself of the secret invitations of Ferdinand, on one side, and the hollow professions and irresolution of the Prince of the Peace, on the other, to advance his troops toward the capital, and to introduce French garrisons in the chief fortresses of the kingdom. Orders for their reception were procured by contrivance or intimidation from the Prince of the Peace himself, and it is said that in some instances they were forged, in others accompanied with private letters from Ferdinand or some military man of his party. It was only where those in command were the reputed enemies of the Prince of the Peace, that such orders were obeyed with any alacrity, and the French received as deliverers and friends. Though no resistance was offered any where, great reluctance, distrust, and ill-humor were shown by those commanders who enjoyed the confidence of the favorite. Murat, Duke of Berg, had indeed secret instructions to take by force any place where admittance was positively refused, and to march as speedily as he could, without spreading great alarm, to Madrid. Not a syllable had been communicated to him of the object of his expedition. When he solicited some explanations for his own guidance upon it, the Emperor wrote a few lines in his own hand to this purpose: "Have I not bid you be at such and such a place by such a day? and reach Madrid before such a time? and what more can a general of my armies require?"

Neither the Emperor nor his agents could have foreseen the events of Aranjuez. They might have supposed that Charles IV. and his court would, like the Prince Regent of Portugal, fly to South America, or that Ferdinand, determined to prevent such a step, would call in French assistance, and fly for protection to the head-quarters of his allies; but it could never be in their contemplation, and still less in their wishes, that the downfall of the Prince of the Peace, the abdication of Charles IV., and the accession of Ferdinand should be effected exclusively by Spaniards. Whether, as some suppose, the subsequent conduct of Napoleon sprang from apprehensions, then first presented to his mind, of a strong national and popular government in Spain, or whether, as more generally conjectured, it was in pursuance of a Machiavelian scheme long conceived and matured, may remain problematical to the biographer and historian. It is certain that the unexpected embarrassment of Beauharnais and the refusal of the Duke of Berg to recognize the new King, disconcerted and disappointed

Ferdinand and his advisers, while the interest taken by the Duke of Berg in the fate of the Prince of the Peace, and the respect shown by him to Charles IV., agreeably surprised the old court. Murat assured me, in 1814, that he had no instructions, and that he suspected Beauharnais of having exceeded his, in the countenance which he gave to the party of Ferdinand both before and after the events at Aranjuez. Nor did any subsequent discoveries change this impression of Murat. On the contrary, his adherents long after that period continued, perhaps from hostility to the name and family of Beauharnais, to profess suspicions of a yet graver nature against the embassador, and to imply that he was actually betraying the interests of the French government to Ferdinand and his party. Charles IV., on the evening of the day on which he abdicated, spoke cheerfully of the step he had taken. He told the diplomatic corps* "that he was tired of business, grown old, and that it was fair his son should take the burden of affairs upon him." But the next morning his tone was entirely altered,† and forty-eight hours had not elapsed before he conveyed his thanks to Murat‡ for withholding his recognition of Ferdinand, and requested him to assure Napoleon that nothing but the dread of confusion and bloodshed would have induced him to acquiesce in the usurpation of his son. The Prince of the Peace had been dragged by the populace of Aranjuez from a hiding hole to which he had somewhat ignominiously retreated. He was

* From Mr. de Bourke, the Danish minister, present.

† De Bourke.

‡ From Count Mosbourg, the confidential friend of Murat, and a clear-headed and accurate man.

insulted, and I believe wounded by one of the rabble, but saved from the more fatal effects of their fury by the intervention of Ferdinand, who exhibited upon that occasion the only trait of talent, spirit, and generosity which relieves the hideous uniformity of his base, cowardly, and perfidious career. "If there be any man here," said he, "who has more reason to be offended with Manuel Godoy than myself, let him take justice into his own hands; but if not, leave me to act as my honor and promise require, and abstain from all violence whatever." With such promptitude did he execute the promise he had given his mother, who, on hearing that her favorite was seized by the populace, conjured her son to fly to his rescue, while his father assured him that he would acquiesce in any thing to prevent bloodshed, and, above all, the murder of the Prince of the Peace. That favorite was conveyed as a prisoner to Madrid, and consigned either there or at the Escurial (I think at the request of Ferdinand himself) to the custody of a French guard. He was afterward removed to Bayonne. Murat, to protect him from insult, conveyed him part of the way in his own carriage, and was shocked, as he told me, at the fear he betrayed, hiding his head, and creeping to the bottom of the carriage whenever they met on the road any body of Spanish soldiers or peasantry. I can believe the story. In truth, the irresolution, vanity, and, above all, the ignorance of Don Manuel Godoy would have incapacitated him for Prime Minister in most countries, and he must have possessed some good and counteracting qualities, both of head and heart, to have retained power so long even in Spain. His ignorance was such that the Chargé d'Affaires* of the Hanseatic Towns, told me that the States he represented were often designated in the superscription or the body of the notes, which he received from the Duke of Alcudia's † office, *Islas Asiaticas*, instead of *Villas Hanseaticas*, and the same person assured me that Godoy was some time Minister of Foreign Affairs before he discovered Prussia and Russia to be two distinct countries; Mr. Sandoz, the Minister from Berlin, being at that time and during the absence of a Russian envoy, the agent for the court of St. Petersburgh at Madrid. As I neither extenuate the vices nor soften the ridicules of this powerful favorite, but recount them as they have been described to me, it is at least fair to record the more favorable impressions which my slight personal intercourse and unimportant transactions with him left of his character on my mind. His manner, though somewhat indolent, or what the French term *nonchalant*, was graceful and attractive. Though he had neither education nor reading, his language was at once elegant and peculiar; and, notwithstanding his humble origin, his whole deportment announced, more than that of any untraveled Spaniard I ever met with, that mixture of dignity, politeness, propriety, and ease, which the habits of good company are supposed exclusively to confer. He seemed born for a high station. Without any effort he would have passed, wherever he was, for the first man in the

* Andreoli, a Venetian by birth, who was also secretary to the Austrian Embassy at Madrid, and himself, though an entertaining mixture of shrewdness and simplicity, very ignorant both of history and geography.

† The Prince of the Peace's title, when Minister of Foreign Affairs

society. I never conversed with him sufficiently to form any judgment of his understanding. Our interviews were mere interchanges of civility. But a transaction of no importance to the public, but of great importance to the parties concerned, took place between us, and he not only behaved with great courtesy to me, but showed both humanity and magnanimity. A young English gentleman of the name of Powell had, before the war between England and Spain, engaged either with General Miranda, or some other South American adventurer, in an expedition to liberate the Spanish colonies. He was taken. By law his life was forfeited, but he was condemned, by a sentence nearly equivalent, to perpetual imprisonment in the unwholesome fortress of Omoa. His father, Chief Justice of Canada, on hearing the sad tidings hastened to England. Unfortunately, hostilities had commenced, under circumstances calculated to exasperate the government and people of Spain. The Chief Justice was, however, determined to try the efficacy of a personal application to alleviate the sufferings of his son, by a change of prison, since he despaired of obtaining his release. Having procured passports, he proceeded to Spain, furnished with a letter of introduction to the Prince of the Peace from me, to whom he applied as recently arrived from thence, and not involved in the angry feelings or discussions which had led to the rupture between the two countries. The Prince received him at Aranjuez, and immediately on reading the letter, and hearing the story, bade the anxious father remain till he had seen the King, and left the room for that purpose without ceremony or delay. He soon returned with an order, not for the change of prison, but for the immediate liberation of the young man. Nor was he satisfied with this act of humanity, but added, with a smile of benevolence, that a parent who had come so far to render a service to his child would like probably to be the bearer of good intelligence himself, and accordingly he furnished him with a passport and permission to sail in a Spanish frigate then preparing to leave Cadiz for the West Indies. When I saw the Prince of the Peace many years afterward at Verona, he lamented to me that his situation would be very precarious if Charles IV. were to die, and he was desirous of ascertaining if he could find an asylum in England. The moment I heard of the event I apprehended, in 1819, I related all the above particulars to Lord Liverpool, and solicited a passport for the Prince of the Peace. Lord Liverpool said, that an English passport to a foreigner implied an invitation, and the government were not prepared to *invite* the Prince of the Peace to England; but he authorized and urged me to assure him that he would be unmolested if he arrived there, and enjoy every protection for his person and property that a foreigner was entitled to. The answer of the Prince of the Peace to my communication of this assurance was concise, and to the following purpose: "He had, for many years, disposed of the resources of one of the richest kingdoms in Europe, he had made the fortune of thousands and thousands, but I was the only mortal who, since his fall, had expressed any sense or shown any recollection of any service, great or small, received from him. I might therefore judge of the pleasure my letter had given him." He did not however come to England.*

* See Appendix, No. III.

The events at Bayonne are very copiously, but somewhat variously related by many Spaniards and Frenchmen, eye-witnesses or actors in those scenes. I had no particular opportunity of hearing details not otherwise known. Indeed, I have dwelt on the previous events in Spain (on which I had collected information from the Duke of Infantado in England, from the King and Queen at Rome, and King Joachim at Naples, as well as from one or two intelligent but indifferent spectators) with some prolixity, because the state of factions at that time has either been grossly misunderstood, or artfully misrepresented by sundry English writers and speakers of apparent authority; and because a more accurate knowledge of them is necessary to enable the future historian of the Spanish war and revolutions to trace the causes and ascertain the bearings of many transactions in the progress of those memorable struggles. A singular circumstance affecting the character of Napoleon, in one of the most questionable passages of his career, is worthy of observation. He knew that the government of Charles IV. had defied him in an open proclamation, he ascertained, on the occupation of Berlin in 1806, that it was promoting a confederacy against France, and he was well aware that as early as 1803 it had secretly fomented a conspiracy against his person, by furnishing the accomplices of Georges with passports to cross the Pyrenees. Yet, in no public paper, nor so far as I know in any private conversation, did he ever allege such facts as motives or excuses for his invasion of Spain, and dethronement of the Bourbon dynasty there. Charles IV. in conversation with me mentioned Bonaparte and his own personal dislike to him more than once. It was whimsical* to hear a man who had lost a crown, descant on the manners, talents, and attainments of the greatest man of the age, who had obtained one, in terms of scorn and disparagement. He could, he said neither talk nor write any language correctly, and he chuckled at his own superiority, by observing, that at Bayonne and elsewhere he, Charles, had kept a diary, an effort of industry and genius, of which he was confident Napoleon was incapable. If the notes of the Royal Exile could be recovered, I suspect they would not raise the literary reputation of the Spanish branch of the House of Bourbon; but as he had been exposed to many vicissitudes, and must have known the secret of many mysterious occurrences, and, as moreover, though unfeeling, brutal, silly, and credulous, he was nevertheless a man of veracity, it is a matter of regret that the MS. on which he plumed himself so greatly, should have fallen into the hands of the Spanish or Roman government, who have in all probability destroyed it. Perhaps the memoirs of the Chevalier Azara, many years embassador at Rome and Paris, and a man of wit, judgment, and sarcasm, shared the same fate. His papers were still at Paris when he died, six months after retiring from office, at Burgos. The French government endeavored to detain them, but some, and among them a History of Italy during his time, were saved by his brother and taken to Spain. If extant, they

* Perhaps not much more so than to hear great princes and kings who have never seen, or, at least, gained a battle, speak in a tone of authority of the mistakes made and the incapacity betrayed by the captain of our age, who has gained the greatest. Some of my contemporaries and countrymen have had, and, perhaps, enjoyed such a diversion.

must be valuable. He was in the habit of recounting with great humor and great accuracy a variety of anecdotes, and he had had access to many of the secrets of the Papal Government. No man was less disposed by temper or opinion to democracy or to France, but the anti-revolutionary war and the conduct of the old governments in Europe, and of England in particular, compelled him to become subservient to both. "Your Mr. Pitt," said he to me in 1802, "resolved, I know not why, that every foreigner should be either a French Jacobin, or a monk of the tenth century. I made my choice with some difficulty and with great concern; and so, you see *me*, a knight of Malta, a servant of his Most Catholic Majesty, embassador and confidential adviser of his Holiness the Pope, covered with Bourbon orders and titles—you see me, I say, here at the age of sixty and upward, the Chevalier Azara of Arragon, a French Jacobin! courting an adventurer at the head of the Republic, and inviting you to dine at the nuptials of his aid-de-camp (Duroc), and all this is because the minister of a Protestant state and parliamentary king determined that any Catholic or Spaniard, who would not submit to be a fanatic, a bigot, a mere friar, or monk, should be considered an enemy of social order, regular government, religion, and *what not!*" There was surely much humor in the picture he drew, and there was truth and philosophy in the lesson it conveyed.

After the battle of Baylen, and the formation of the Central Junta in Spain, I again visited that country, with my family. The Junta had been hastily chosen, and was composed of materials not happily assorted to one another. The members were driven from Aranjuez before they were well installed in their seats, before they had clearly defined their authority, and before they had traced the system of government they intended to establish. I saw them at Seville; they were too much occupied with the ceremonies, forms, and patronage of their new government. They had, indeed, among them some ex-ministers and magistrates of great integrity, enlightened views, and distinguished talents. Among these, Don Gaspar Melchor de Jovellanos was the most eminent; but even they, from the caution of their time of life, and from the habits of magistracy, were somewhat too scrupulously observant of technical rules inapplicable to the exigency of circumstances, and too readily alarmed at those vigorous measures of innovation which a state of revolution and civil war demands. Their choice of ministers did them credit. The venerable Saavedra was among them, and Hermida, a still older man, who was Minister of Grace and Justice, though both prejudiced and capricious, was a man of knowledge, courage, and capacity. Garay, who, though member of the Junta, presided over their foreign affairs, combined zeal and discernment with more knowledge of the world and amenity of manner than is usual in Spanish politicians. His office in the Alcazar was the resort of a small society or club, called la Junta Chica,* which direct-

* The Duke of Altamira, Marquis of Astorga, was the least man I ever saw in society, and smaller than many dwarfs exhibited for money. He was President of the Junta, and drove about with guards like a royal personage. They called him the *Rey Chico*, a name formerly given to a king of Grenada, and it was in allusion to that nickname that the small club or knot of men I have mentioned, gave themselves that of *Junta Chica*.

ed the insurrectionary press, and was active, both in public and in private, in promoting a convocation of Cortes, the promulgation of liberal and tolerant laws, and the establishment of a popular government. It was composed of young men of more ardor and imagination than experience or prudence, who had imbibed their notions of freedom from the encyclopedists of France, rather than from the history of their ancient institutions, or from the immediate wants of their own country. They were, perhaps, more competent to exhibit their own contempt of superstition and disdain of abuses, than to reconcile either the Church or the nobility to a rational correction of them, and to render those powerful bodies instrumental, first in the recovery of independence, and afterward in the establishment of the freedom of their country. The crude projects of this rising party, on one hand, and equally impolitic, and, perhaps, less honest irresolution of the Junta in convoking the Cortes, on the other, contributed to widen the breach between those who had concurred in resisting the French from different and even opposite motives. Hence, when the Cortes did meet, some deputies were more intent on destroying the power of the Church, and suppressing the privileges of the nobility, than on resisting the common enemy; and others were more jealous of such designs, as aiming at a revolution in the internal government, than averse to the abuses, or even to the foreigners, who threatened their national independence. The popular orators, mistaking the applause of Cadiz, that least aristocratical and least devout city in Spain, for the opinion of the nation, naturally caressed the former rather that the latter party. Hence their proceedings, and even the constitution they framed assumed a character little congenial to the wishes or wants of the people they represented, though exempt from many of those errors of extravagant democracy and anti-monarchical contrivances, which, some years afterward, were ignorantly and maliciously urged against them throughout Europe. The most prominent were Don Agustin Arguelles and the Marquis of Matarrosa, both natives and deputies of the Asturies. I knew Arguelles when a very young man, at Oviedo, in 1793. He came afterward to England, in 1806, on some secret mission, which the events* of that year prevented him from executing or avowing. He remained in a state of ill health in London till the Spanish revolution; and when about to embark at Portsmouth for Lisbon, he met and returned with Don Andres de la Vega and Matarrosa, who had suddenly arrived from the Asturies, charged with a mission for the English government from the spirited insurgents of the little town of Oviedo. He was a man of reading and reflection, and had studied our literature and our history with great success during his residence in London, though accidental circustances gave him a very false and unfavorable impression of the foreign policy of England. On the very first opening of the Cortes he acquired a great ascendant over his colleagues; he soon became the leader of the popular party in that assembly. The passion for applause so dangerous and so seductive to every orator,

* Particularly the battle of Jena; for I suspect (though I do not know), that his mission was connected with the plan of a confederacy with the Northern Powers against France; that plan was discomfited by the defeat of the Russians, but the participation of Spain therein was detected, as I have before observed, by the French at Berlin.

and a propensity to suspicion, unfortunately prevalent in the mind of most Spaniards wherever foreigners are concerned, led him, perhaps, to commit many errors as a legislator and a statesman. In every impartial history of those times, Arguelles must bear his share of the blame which attaches to the mistakes in the constitution, to the ill-timed distrust of Lord Wellington and the English, and to the unjust and impolitic treatment of the American colonies; yet his unblemished integrity, and the dignified earnestness of his eloquence, were even then acknowledged, and raised the Cortes in the estimation of Europe. He was afterward exposed to the severer trials of adversity; and, notwithstanding his delicate health, he bore the sufferings which the inhuman and ungrateful Ferdinand inflicted on his benefactors and supporters, with equanimity and fortitude. For eighteen months was he immured in the unwholesome atmosphere of a prison, within the guard-house of Madrid, deprived of books, pen and ink, and nearly of light, and debarred from all intercourse but with his jailers; unconscious of all that was passing about him except the riot and drunkenness of the soldiery, the occasional remonstrances of his fellow-sufferers, Martinez de la Rosa and Manuel Quintana, who were the tenants of similar adjoining rooms, and on one occasion the festivities of the King himself, who had the brutality to give a banquet over the dungeons, or at least within the hearing of the victims of his cruelty. Arguelles was afterward removed to a fortress on the coast of Africa, Melilla. The comparative mildness of his treatment there was to be attributed to the sympathy of the garrison, the humanity of the governor, and the intercession of his friends, not to any remorse in Ferdinand. The subsequent career of Arguelles is well known. During his ministry, and while the Cortes continued, Ferdinand distinguished him from his associates by marked dislike, thereby manifesting his discernment in discovering the qualities most formidable to tyranny; viz., consistency of principle, firmness of spirit, and austerity of virtue in public and private.

Matarrosa was hardly twenty years old, when he brought the news of the massacre of the 2d of May at Madrid to the little capital of the Asturies; with unexampled rapidity prevailed on the people of the principality to revolt, and conveyed the intelligence, together with an application for assistance, to England. He was thus early initiated in public affairs. His youth and services combined with considerable natural endowments to make him a favorite with the first Cortes at Cadiz. He was surely more pardonable than many of his colleagues, if he was as inconsiderate as any in courting popularity, and if he preferred for a season the warm applauses of the people to the more sober approbation of his judicous countryman, Andres de la Vega. On the return of Ferdinand, he escaped from Spain, and was in his absence condemned to death. He resided in France till the re-establishment of the Spanish Constitution in 1820, when he became first a minister, and afterward an active and useful member of the Cortes. Experience had improved his talents, and moderated without changing his principles; but his habits at Paris, and his frequent visits to that city, somewhat injured his popularity. Moreover, the fortune which he had inherited, and which he, perhaps, improved during his administration, rendered him, like the soldier of Lucullus, less eager to mount the breach than he had been at the outset of his career. He had, indeed, retired some time before the war of 1823 was apprehended, and was consulted by the Duke of Wellington when he passed through Paris, in 1822, to Verona. On that occasion he acknowledged the defects of the Constitutión, but deprecated the notion of rectifying them by foreign intimidation. When the war broke out he withdrew to England; and, since its fatal conclusion, has returned to Paris, where, if somewhat more of an Atticus than a Cato, he is exempt from the reproach of changing any principles, or truckling to any enemy in power.

The celebrity of the Spanish generals in the revolutionary war is not sufficient to excite much curiosity about their personal qualifications and history, nor would my opportunities enable me to satisfy it. I knew little of them. The Marquis of Romana, more of a soldier than a general, was a good scholar, and had some originality of character. After a good education at Sorreze, he had distinguished himself by his courage during war, and by strange adventures with gipsies in company with Lord Mount Stuart during peace. He had a strong predilection for every thing English; he rescued his army from Denmark with great address, and was always a favorite with the soldiery, because he cheerfully shared all their hardships, and sincerely partook of their antipathy to the French. General Blake, the most *ill-starred** of commanders, was highly accomplished in his profession, and

* In more than one of his well-written dispatches, he speaks of his *Mala Estrella.* I am in possession of his MS. of his first campaign in Old Castile and Biscay, and General Foy who read it at Holland House, when intending to write a history of the Spanish war, assured me that it was the work of an accomplished officer.

remarkable for retaining, in spite of uniform disaster, great influence over the officers of the Spanish army. His wife, when Coruña was taken, took refuge in Plymouth. She thought herself neglected by our Government; and that circumstance confirmed the prejudices against England which an Irish extraction had entailed on General Blake. He fomented in Spaniards the ill-timed jealousy of their allies, which long impeded, and nearly counteracted, all success against the common enemy.

General Castaños had grown old in a court, and was more adapted for it than for a camp. Hot weather, the plunder and baggage with which the French had encumbered themselves, and the self-sufficiency of their commander, gained for him the victory of Baylen. He had the good sense and modesty to ascribe his success to those circumstances. The French general, Dupont, had the bad taste to preserve his vanity even in his chagrin. When he delivered his sword to Castaños he said: "You may well, General, be proud of this day; it is remarkable that I have never lost a pitched battle till now—I, who have been in more than twenty, and gained them all." "It is the more remarkable," replied dryly the sarcastic Spaniard, "because I never was in one before in my life."

Albuquerque was reckoned to have capacity in the field. Off it, he certainly had none. The strictures on his conduct agitated him so much that he sat up three nights, without food or sleep, framing an answer to them, and died, with the assistance of Père Elisée, a French physician, in a paroxysm of fever and despair.

I never saw La Cuesta, Ballesteros, or O'Donnel.*

* Abisbal.

The first was described as a curious and almost ludicrous specimen of an impracticable Spaniard. He was eighty years old when he was appointed to the command—haughty, suspicious, ignorant, and obstinate, but patient of fatigue, alike incapable of artifice or fear, and so pedantically observant of the forms of honor, that he would sacrifice to punctilio his own interests and glory and the cause in which he was engaged, deeming it a less disgrace to lose ten battles, than to alter dispositions once approved, or to yield the smallest tittle in etiquette to an inferior officer or a foreign ally. Ballesteros, though he had originally risen from the ranks of an irregular force, partook of the same spirit, but he was of a more active, or at least docile age, and proved himself an able partisan; and, notwithstanding subsequent appearances to the contrary, was, I believe, sincerely zealous in the service of his country. Not so O'Donnel: he retained more of the nation from which he sprang, than of that in which he was born, and educated to arms. He showed, indeed, greater talent, and had more success than all the other Spanish generals; but he was unsteady, intemperate, and unreasonable, and regardless of truth and character.

Among the chiefs of guerillas, Lord Wellington had the highest opinion of Mina, who justified that preference by his subsequent conduct. He had in truth a great fund of mother wit in all things,* as well as courage, activity, and the *coup d'œil* in war.

The most judicious choice, or rather the most fortunate

* What the Spaniards call strangely enough *Gramatica Parda*, tawny grammar, knowledge and tact without reading. I have heard it applied to Mina; and I translate it *mother wit*.

accident for the confederate war in the Peninsula, was the appointment of Don Miguel Alava, as the channel of communication between the English head-quarters and the Spanish government. He had the advantage, no small one in Spain, of a naval education. He had seen service, and yet was conversant with the manners and character of the court. His gallantry, openness, and good nature soon ingratiated him with the English army, and gained him the confidence and friendship of Lord Wellington. He had some of the prejudices, but none of the suspicions of his countrymen. Impetuous in temper, and heedless in conversation, he was yet so honest, so natural, so cheerful and so affectionate, that the most reserved man could scarcely have given less offense than he who commanded the respect and won the affections of so many by his intrepid openness and sincerity. He was imprisoned on the first return of Ferdinand to Spain, and released only at the personal intercession of Lord Wellington. He was then named embassador to the Netherlands, but had returned and was living in retirement at Vittoria when the Constitution was for a second time adopted in Spain. It was a great oversight in the governments which succeeded not to send him embassador to London. At one time the pedantry of not employing a deputy, at another the wish of rewarding the Duke of Frias (a strange little man, not devoid of spirit, but quite unfit for such a place), induced them to neglect so obvious and so useful a choice. Alava would, I am persuaded, have convinced the Duke of Wellington of the propriety and practicability of preventing a French invasion of Spain. He would possibly have rescued his country from the calamities, and, what is worse, the dishonor which has ensued. Fully aware of the defects of the Constitution, General Alava felt the ignominy of altering it at the menace of foreigners, and nobly adhered to the cause of his country. Ferdinand, when conveyed by him to Port Sta. Maria, invited him earnestly to stay, but Alava judiciously distrusted his sincerity, and somewhat bluntly reminded him that he had been thrown in prison in consequence of relying on his moderation before. He escaped to Gibraltar, and sailed from thence to England. The Duke of Wellington received him cordially and generously. The same qualities which had endeared him to our officers, rendered him popular with London society. He was welcome every where except at court. George IV., who wears his crown in virtue of the exclusion of the Stuarts, affected not to forgive a Spaniard for concurring in a moment of national danger in the temporary dethronement of a king more unwarlike than James I., more perfidious than either Charles, and more arbitrary and cruel than James II.

I know little of Portugal or Portuguese that would have the interest of novelty to English readers. The king and queen, very opposite in principle, character, and conduct, have a natural abhorrence of one another. They, in truth, have nothing in common but a revolting ugliness of person and a great awkwardness of manner. He is well meaning, but weak and cowardly, and so apprehensive of being governed by his ostensible ministers, that he becomes the victim of low and obscure cabals, and renders his councils at all times unsteady, irresolute, and uncertain. The Queen's outrageous zeal in the cause of despotism, miscalled legitimacy, is supposed to have softened his aversion to a representative Assembly and a constitutional form of government. The Queen is vindictive, ambitious, and selfish, and has strong propensities to every species of intrigue, political or amorous.

In general, the leading men in Portugal are not deficient in talents or knowledge. Vanity in them often acts the part of more enlightened patriotism; but they are full of little jealousies and artifices, and more cunning in their negotiations with powerful states than wise in the management of their own. Araujo, a man of capacity, hoped by cajoling England and France, to elude the designs of both, and thus ended by leaving Portugal in the possession of one, and his sovereign and the Brazils entirely at the mercy of the other. Souza, Count Funchal, anxious to assimilate the institutions of his country to those of England, and sincerely attached to the House of Braganza, contrived to pass his life in squabbling with and persecuting the Reformers, and to lose the favor of his sovereign by declining the office which alone could enable him to execute his designs. Yet his notions were just and enlightened; but with good abilities he took injudicious and indirect ways to enforce them. He consequently failed, and had need of that cheerfulness of temper and pleasantry in conversation in which he abounded, to console him for the many political and personal disappointments to which he was exposed.

I never was in Russia, and I merely passed through Austria in the spring of 1796. Their governments and leading men are nearly unknown to me.

It has been the fashion to describe the Emperor Francis

II.* as a mild, benevolent man, who, without shining parts, had sound notions of justice, and great disposition to exercise it impartially and mercifully. It may be so. But to all appearance, in all relations of life he has acted like a person of a character directly the reverse. As he received an education unusually philosophical for a prince, his mistakes can not be ascribed to that ignorance and prejudice which are so often but so strangely urged as palliations of the crimes of royalty. At the commencement of his reign he imprisoned, like felonious subjects, in contempt of the law, or at least the usage of civilized nations, his enemies,

* 1837. Since writing these strictures on the character of Francis II. of Austria, I have seen Federico Confalonieri. He was illegally arrested and condemned to death by an iniquitous sentence, about 1823. The punishment was commuted, by a mockery of mercy (itself wrung with some difficulty from the Emperor by the Empress and other ladies of fashion), into close and for the most part solitary imprisonment of fifteen years in a Moravian fortress! Confalonieri ascribes his persecution, and, above all, the unusual and relentless severity of his imprisonment to the cruelty of two persons, Metternich and the Emperor himself. But he justly remarks, that the greater portion of the crime (and such horrid acts of power are crimes) must, in all presumptive reasoning, be charged on the Emperor. Prince Metternich's power survived his master; and yet on the death of that sovereign, Confalonieri was immediately released from his prison, and allowed to seek safety in banishment. In this mitigation, Metternich not only acquiesced, but was disposed to relax, and did afterward concur in relaxing, even some remaining parts of the sentence. Let not the princes of unlimited monarchy take the benefit of maxims applicable only to constitutional kings. Acts of baseness and cruelty perpetrated under them are *their own* and not their advisers'—the fruit of that selfishness and obduracy which their station naturally engenders, and which it generally produces in abundance.

civil or military, whether found with or without arms in their hands, and whether taken on neutral or hostile territory. Witness Semonville, Maret,* Beurnonville, Lafayette, and his companions. At the age of twenty-two, he had the heart to tell the wife of the latter, a woman of unblemished virtue, in the discharge of an heroic duty, that he would allow her to join her husband, but on the condition that she was never to quit the prison in which she visited him. He received the papers of the French deputies at Rastadt, *murdered within his lines*, without insisting on the detection and punishment of the murderers. He either consented to sacrifice his daughter to the cowardly policy of propitiating an usurper and a tyrant, or he basely abandoned and dethroned the prince whom he had selected for his son-in-law. He separated his daughter from her husband, and helped to disinherit his grandson, the issue of a marriage he had certainly sanctioned, and I believe earnestly solicited. With a view of estranging the same daughter from her exiled and deposed husband, whose conduct to her was irreproachable, he is said to have encouraged, and even contrived her infidelities. Unlike his uncle and father, he checks the genius and restrains the liberties of his Italian subjects. Yet his

* The two first, employed on a diplomatic mission, were seized on neutral territory, and during their captivity of twenty-two months were treated frequently more like malefactors than prisoners of war, though, in truth, they were neither. They had actually fetters. It should always be recollected that these crimes were committed, not in countries in a state of revolution or civil war, but in *regular hereditary monarchies*, professedly fighting for the cause of religion, social order, law, and subordination!

alternate usurpation and abandonment, barter and resumption of those territories must have taught them to consider allegiance as a mere question of convenience; and the Emperor must be satisfied that he has himself been instrumental in dispelling those illusions which he has of late endeavored to impose by severity on mankind. Prince Metternich bears, no doubt, a share of the odium attached to such measures; but it is unjust to acquit the principal in order to load the accessory.* That minister, originally a partisan of the French faction, and then a tool of Napoleon, has, no doubt, since the fall of that great prince, supported the system which succeeded him. He seems hardly qualified by any superior genius to assume the ascendency in the councils of his own and neighboring nations, which common rumor has for some years attributed to him. He appeared to me, in the very short intercourse I had with him, little superior to the common run of continental politicians and courtiers, and clearly inferior to the Emperor of Russia in those qualities which secure an influence in great affairs. Some who admit the degrading, but too prevalent opinion that a disregard of truth is useful and necessary in the government of mankind, have, on that score, maintained the contrary proposition. His manners are reckoned insinuating. In my slight acquaintance with him in London, I was not struck with them; they seemed such as might have been expected from a German who had studied French vivacity in the fashionable novels

* I have heard it observed, and I believe justly, that the Emperor passed, during his long reign, for a weak, foolish, but good sort of man; but that he deserved none of these epithets. He was a man of some understanding, little feeling, and no justice.

of the day. I saw little of a sagacious and observant statesman, or of a courtier accustomed to very refined and enlightened society.*

The address of Alexander himself, the Emperor of Russia, was, perhaps, liable to a similar criticism. But he was obviously well educated, and had a desire to please, founded not merely on vanity, but on a higher sense of duty, and a real good nature in his disposition. Napoleon, who had trusted too far to the ascendency he had at one time assumed over his mind, accused him, when emancipated from his control, of matchless artifice and duplicity,† "C'est un véritable caractère Grec" (said he to Lord Ebrington at Elba), words which, in the mouth of a Corsican, imply the summit of treachery and deceit. But unsteadiness and inconsistency are not necessary proofs of insincerity. Alexander was placed by birth in a station, and received from Laharpe an education infinitely beyond the scope of intellect with which nature had endowed him.

* His dispatches and public papers of late years (I write this note in 1837,) have assumed the character of elaborate and subtle dissertations on public law, or rhetorical exercises even to pedantry.

† Pozzo di Borgo, though far from stigmatizing such conduct as Greek duplicity, as did Bonaparte, concurred, however, with his countryman in representing Alexander as acting a part throughout. He was never, he said, the dupe of Bonaparte, he always distrusted and always meant to subvert his power. Notwithstanding this testimony, I adhere to my opinion, and think Alexander's admiration and devotion were, for a time, unfeigned. Subsequent events in his career show he was susceptible of such feelings, and it was not unnatural on his revival of intimacy with Napoleon's bitter enemy to disclaim the weakness of having ever been his dupe. It was what a weak man, in such circumstances, would naturally do.

Such disproportion between the natural capacity and accidental contents of a man's mind might well create some confusion and irregularity. Moreover, the Emperor had a dash of romance, and some constitutional predisposition to mental derangement, which unlimited power and the vicissitude of great affairs are particularly apt to bring into action. I have little doubt that his admiration for Napoleon was unfeigned, and blended in his mind with some mysterious notion that Providence had created him as his coadjutor and guide. When, therefore, at the theatre at Erfurt* he roused him, and seized his hand with enthusiasm, on hearing from the stage that

> "L'amitié d'un grand homme est un bienfait des cieux,"

he was not vying with the talents of the great actor who uttered the sentiment, but honestly and unaffectedly giving way to what was then his own. It was, however, during that memorable interview, that Alexander began to be somewhat alarmed at the projects and even nettled at the behavior of Napoleon. Talleyrand,† from a questionable preference of the interests of peace to the official duties of his confidential station, ventured secretly to apprise the Emperor of Russia that the object of the interview was to engage him in a confederacy against Austria, and even went so far as to advise him to avoid coming to Erfurt, or, if he did, to resist firmly the instances of Napoleon

* Marshal Soult, who was in the theatre, and witnessed the scenes told me that Napoleon was half asleep or dozing, when Alexander seized his hand with emotion, and observed, that that fine line seemed to be addressed to himself, he felt the application of it, &c.

† From a sincere and correct, but indiscreet friend of Talleyrand's.

to make war upon Austria. On his arrival there, he had, no doubt, frequent opportunities of communicating with Talleyrand, and that minister's sentiments, highly flattering to Alexander,* were not calculated, nor perhaps intended, to rivet or to perpetuate his confidence in Napoleon. Some differences, amounting to altercations, took place; and though Alexander probably did not alter his opinion, and certainly did not openly change his policy, he yet left Erfurt less satisfied with his great ally, and less confidently attached to his system, then he had been at his arrival there. Still his predilections continued, and it was not till irresistible necessity separated him from the policy enjoined by Napoleon, that the rupture between France and Russia occurred. Had Napoleon been less unreasonable in his projects, or less peremptory in exacting every onerous condition of the treaties he had imposed upon Russia, he would probably have retained the ascendency he had assumed over the councils and mind of Alexander; and had Alexander been really and literally as powerful as his title of "Autocrat" supposes, he would not certainly have reverted to the same state of dependence after the capture of Moscow as that he had submitted to ever since the conferences of Tilsit.

The remonstrances of his allies, and of Bernadotte in particular, the resolution of the army † not to acquiesce

* When the conferences at Erfurt had closed, and the two carriages were drawn up to the door in different directions to convey the two Emperors to their respective dominions, Talleyrand whispered to Alexander, as he went down stairs, "*Ah, si Votre Majesté pouvoit se tromper de voiture!*"

† Sir Robert Wilson; confirmed by other testimony and many

in any peace he should sign, manifested in no equivocal manner, and the concurring murmurs of the nobility, and even of his own family, together with numberless uncontrollable circumstances, overruled his inclination, rescued him from the councils of pusillanimity, and converted him, in spite of his will and his nature, into a conqueror and a hero. But I have explained the occurrences of that time elsewhere.* The rapid turn of fortune which ensued, must have convinced him that no unalterable destiny had enchained Victory to the car of the French Emperor. It was pardonable and even amiable in him to be dazzled with the popularity which rewarded the affability of his manners and the comparative forbearance of his councils on his first occupation of Paris in 1814. It required at that time all the persuasion and art of Pozzo di Borgo (and few men ever possessed a larger share of both those commodities), as well as a coincidence of fortuitous circumstances, to prevail on him to acquiesce in the forced restoration of the Bourbons. When I saw him in England, and for many months afterward, he was much taken with what he called "*Idées libérales.*"† He

circumstances. One might add, that about and from this time that lively, dexterous, and able man, Pozzo di Borgo, was active in rendering Alexander, through the means of persuasion and intrigue, irreconcilable with Napoleon.

* Vide Chap. vii. Part i. A of my MS. Memoirs.

† He not only talked "liberal language," but courted the "Liberal party," at that time in a way which, if it did not prove great levity and great unsteadiness, must have proceeded from yet worse qualities in his disposition, and such as are described in Rulhiere's History of Poland as the chief ingredients in Russian policy. Lafayette told me that he met Alexander at Madame de Stael's; he took him aside, and

had not indeed reduced them to "*Idées nettes*," either in his conversation or his understanding, but they gave him a notion of imposing representative constitutions on other countries, and even of preparing his own for the reception of some reforms tending that way. The atmosphere of Vienna, and the discussions about Poland, soon afterward damped his ardor for popularity. Surprise, indignation, and fear at the sudden return of Napoleon in 1815, placed him at the head of the opposite party in the ensuing war and subsequent treaties. A mixture of policy and superstition suggested the Holy Alliance. Alexander blended some mysterious notions of duty toward God with schemes of worldly policy, tyranny, and ambition. He was at that time in some measure under the dominion of a Livonian lady, Madame Krudner, who after some celebrity acquired in her earlier years by the beauty of her person and the freedom of her pen, had become a visionary and devotee, and either pretended or imagined that she could divine the intentions of

complained of the narrow prejudices and bad conduct of "*vos Bourbons.*" Lafayette observed they were not *his*, but hoped that misfortune and experience might have corrected their errors. "Du tout," replied the Muscovite philosopher and Emperor; "ils ne sont ni corrigés, ni corrigibles." Lafayette, though somewhat unwilling to prolong such a conversation, could not resist asking him why, with such an impression of their incapacity, he had bestowed them on France. "Ce n'étoit pas moi," replied Alexander, "ils sont venus comme *une inondation*, l'un de Nancy, l'autre de l'Angleterre." The last assertion was false in fact. It has certainly the appearance of a design in Alexander to take merit with the Liberals for what he knew he did not deserve; and favors Napoleon's view of the duplicity of his character.

Providence. Alexander, it is true, was soon prevailed upon to remove her from his presence, but he continued liable to, and was perhaps never entirely exempt from, illusions of supernatural agency* on the events of the world, and on his conduct in particular. He, for instance, wrote in his own hand a letter of invitation to an ignorant visionary woman † in the Pyrenees, who had pretended to the gift of prophecy. Other traits of credulity and superstition have been related to me by persons well acquainted with the secrets of his court. A morbid reverence for Napoleon had made him long adhere to a policy, which, under the name of the Continental System, was at variance with the wishes and interests of his subjects: an honest, but perhaps equally morbid sense of duty led him latterly to espouse a principle, which, under the name of legitimacy, required the sacrifice of the national prejudices, and the surrender of the favorite project of the Russian cabinet to the preservation of the Turk, that

* Talleyrand told me (18th Oct. 1830), that Louis XVIII. refused his consent to a marriage between the Duke of Berry and a sister of Alexander, from a persuasion that in the Imperial family of Russia the malady of insanity was hereditary.

† Her name was *Madame Bouche*. She pretended to have seen the Archangel Michael. She was conveyed to St. Petersburgh, and remained there some time, lodged and boarded at the Emperor's expense. I am not quite sure of the fact of his writing to her in his own hand, though it was so related to me. I have been since informed that some agent or embassador was instructed to write to her, and furnish her with the means of proceeding to St. Petersburgh. Such particulars are immaterial, the main part of the story is true—he consulted her. She was past fifty years old, and he had never seen her till he sent for her.

natural enemy of his country, and persecutor of his religion.

In the internal government of his vast empire, if not uniformly consistent and judicious, he was at least free from all taint of injustice, cruelty, or revenge—no slight commendation of a man in possession of unlimited power for nearly a quarter of a century over many millions of his fellow-creatures, and in a country inured and familiarized to iniquities and atrocities of every kind in their rulers. That he was an accomplice in the *murder* of his father has not been proved, and probably is not literally true. That according to the strict maxims of political morality, which he affected to impose upon others, he was a sort of accessory after the fact can not well be disputed. He not only accepted the crown, which devolved on him in consequence of a crime, but he left the criminals unquestioned and unpunished. He even admitted some of them, such as Bennigsen, the actual assassin, to commands of great trust and importance. Pahlen his chief adviser, certainly knew,* and in all likelihood communicated to him that a project was on foot to compel Paul to abdicate or to submit to great restraints on his authority. If they were not both aware of particulars, it was prudence, delicacy, and choice alone that kept them in ignorance. The names of the conspirators were known to them. Alexander, though young, was not so unversed in the history or so ignorant of the manners of his country,

* I had *proof* of this from a man of integrity in the confidence of Pahlen; and from the same authority, I heard many particulars of the conspiracy, the assassination, and the effects of it, which I have preserved among my papers, and which have been since confirmed by other testimony.

nor so deficient in common sagacity as not to conjecture what must be the termination of a successful conspiracy against an Autocrat. He foresaw the tendency, and winked at the progress of the plot; he knew the violence, but consented to reap the fruits of the catastrophe. On the other hand, before we condemn him, we must weigh well many circumstances in excuse or palliation of the degree of connivance which can be fixed upon him. In the first place, he had reasons to entertain apprehensions not only for his own immediate safety, but for that of his mother, whom he tenderly loved. He witnessed every day the misery inflicted by the frenzy of Paul on individuals, and he could not be ignorant that it threatened to involve the empire in confusion and ruin. Justice and humanity called for the extinction of a nuisance of such vast and increasing magnitude. There is no mitigation of the excesses of despotism; violence alone can remove them. Those, therefore, who are in contact with such disorders must, both in principle and practice, be more familiarized with forcible remedies, and more pardonable for applying them, than persons who never have to deal with symptoms so outrageous. The assassination of an emperor, even by members of his own family, is no uncommon occurrence in Russia or Turkey. It can not, perhaps it ought not, to excite the same horror there as in more refined and civilized societies. Acquiescence, or even participation in plots of assassination, is not a crime of the same dye in despotic countries as in those where the force of law and the mildness of manners render such bloody expedients unusual and unnecessary. Had Alexander denounced the plot, or even merely defeated the execution of it, he would, in truth, only have postponed an event which was inevitable, and in all probability he must either have fallen in the interval a victim to his father's suspicion, or ultimately have shared his fate in order to secure the impunity of the conspirators.

Such scenes justly excite the abhorrence of good men; but it is not against the actors, but against the system which creates and in some sort requires such guilt, that their indignation should be directed. It has been a fashion of late years, and one much sanctioned by the prince in question, to consider legitimacy and hereditary right to power as nearly synonymous. But legitimacy, if it means any thing, implies a respect and honor for law. Now there is no scheme of government in which the laws of God and nature are so necessarily violated, and in which, practically, those of mankind are so frequently subverted, as in hereditary despotism. In the early part of his reign Count Pahlen had great influence with Alexander; but Count Woronzow betrayed to the young sovereign the low opinion which that minister had formed of his master's talents, and which, in the confidence of old friendship, he had imprudently communicated to his countryman in London. Pahlen was dismissed. Whispers, that his suspected participation in the plot which deprived Paul of his throne and his life, made his ostensible power indelicate and offensive, served to conceal the real reason of his retirement. Czartorinsky, who succeeded him, was equally distinguished for abilities and for pure and lofty disinterestedness of character. His ministry was not fortunate, but he contributed in no slight degree to infuse into the minds of the Emperor and Empress, and indeed of the whole court, more elevated and enlightened notions for the government both of Poland and

Russia than had hitherto found their way into the cabinet of St. Petersburgh. To him, after Laharpe, Russia and the world are chiefly indebted for such benefits as they have derived from the prevalence of humane principles in the mind of Alexander. But Czartorinsky was a Pole, exposed to the jealousy and suspicion of the Russians, and perhaps too much occupied, for a prudent man, in providing for the welfare, and redressing the grievances of his native country. He lost his influence in the councils, but not his hold on the affections of Alexander, on the failure of the confederacy in 1805. After the peace of Tilsit, he retired from public employment, and he probably did not ingratiate himself with the court of St. Petersburgh by the earnestness and zeal with which he urged the restoration of Poland, upon the resettlement of Europe in 1814. Alexander, endeavoring to imitate Napoleon, vainly imagined that he could administer every branch of public affairs throughout his vast dominions. His intentions were pure, his impartiality unquestionable, but he had neither sagacity nor knowledge enough to secure him from the consequences of misrepresentation, or the errors of ignorance. His assiduity was indeed sufficient to injure his health and *impair his mind*, but quite inadequate to the pressure of business. Delays, amounting to denial of justice, often ensued. Real grievances were accumulating, and murmurs and complaints* were increasing at the time of his death. If his accession proves how little security princes derive from

* Alexander was perhaps at no period of his reign either so popular or so *secure* in Russia, as the apparent glory of his achievements seemed to denote, or as foreigners imagined. Marshal Soult told me that when at Tilsit, he (Soult) was apprised of a very extensive con-

unlimited power, his administration showed that the best and rarest qualities of a sovereign are insufficient to insure the welfare of his people under the preposterous system which invests him, in right of his birth, with the whole power of the state.

Such prodigious intellects as those of Cæsar or Napoleon seem at first sight to offer exceptions to the remark. But when or where have Cæsars or Napoleons been born or bred in a palace? Is it clear that both those miraculous men, with minds adequate to the stupendous task of governing vast masses of their fellow creatures by their sole will and pleasure, had not other qualities necessarily associated with such active spirits and ardent genius, which, if uncontrolled by law, would counteract and overbalance the benefits their vigilance and discernment were capable of conferring on mankind?

Those who peruse the following pages, traced certainly by no hostile pen, will probably discover the features of such a character, even in the outlines that I am enabled to preserve of the greatest prodigy of the times to which my notices relate—Napoleon Bonaparte.

spiracy against him, in which Bennigsen, the assassin of his father, and the commander of his army, was concerned. Soult, before he had consulted his own government on the matter, disclosed the whole in a private letter to Alexander, and mentioned the names of the conspirators. He showed me the answer of Alexander, in his own handwriting. He thanks Soult in it very warmly for the information, for he says it will be of great use to him, though he does not believe that the matter is quite so important (*tout-à-fait si conséquent*) as the Marshal supposes. Soult added to me with some bitterness, that the letter should some day appear, together with that in which the same Alexander refused him an asylum in his dominions.

I proceed to transcribe some hasty and rambling notes taken when the news of his death reached me at Paris in 1821. They contain a faithful picture of impressions made upon my mind at that time. The reader will indeed remark that I had little personal intercourse with Napoleon; but he will estimate the opportunities I had of conversing with those most capable of giving me information more easily than if I had reduced my notes to a more regular and methodical narrative. I have, however, omitted such facts as I have subsequently had reason to believe untrue, and also such, on the other hand, as have appeared in print on as good or better authority than my own.

The Emperor Napoleon died at St. Helena on the 5th of May, 1821. Some hours before the news was generally known in Paris, a note in pencil was left at my door, without signature or date, directed to Lady Holland, and apprising her shortly,* but with concern, of the event. The intelligence had been conveyed from Calais by telegraph. Few days elapsed before Lady Holland received the two following letters from Sir Hudson Lowe:

"St. Helena, 6th May, 1821.

"Dear Madam,

"The compassionate interest which your Ladyship has so constantly and in so generous a manner shown toward the remarkable person who had been so long under my charge, imposes it as a duty on me to take the earliest opportunity of informing you that he breathed his last yesterday evening at about ten minutes before six o'clock.

* I think the words were:

"Le grand homme est mort."

See Appendix, No. IV.

The public accounts render it unnecessary for me to enter into any particular details as to the causes of his death. His father died of the same complaint, a scirrhous cancer of the stomach, near what is called the pylorus. It was beyond the power of medicine to have saved him. Every assistance which the means of this island could afford was tendered to him. He appeared conscious of his approaching fate, and would receive the visits of only one English medical person in addition to his own medical attendant, Professor Antommarchi. He died without appearing to suffer much pain. Praying my best respects to Lord Holland, I remain,

"Your Ladyship's most obliged
"and faithful servant,
(Signed) "H. Lowe."

"To the Rt. Hon. The Lady Holland."

"St. Helena, 15th May, 1821.

"Dear Madam,

"On looking over the effects left by Bonaparte, in company with Count Montholon and Marchand, his valet de chambre, I observed two snuff-boxes of wrought gold, one of them with a cameo of very large size set in the cover of it, representing a goat with a fawn riding upon it, nibbling at some grapes on a vine stalk. Count Montholon informed me it had been a present from Pope Pius VII.* to Bonaparte at the peace of Tolentino. The other box was of a plainer kind, and had simply an N engraved or rather cut in with the point of some sharp instrument on the top of it. After some time had passed in looking at various other things in the apartment, I returned to the spot

* Sic in MS., a mistake for Pius the *Sixth*.

where the boxes lay, and taking up the first of them to admire the beauty of the cameo, I afterward opened the lid of it, when I observed a card at the bottom of the box exactly cut to its size, and the following words in Bonaparte's own hand written upon it: "L'Empereur Napoleon à Lady Holland, témoignage de satisfaction et d'estime." On the back of the card was written in another hand: Donné par le Pape Pius VII.* à Tolentino, 1797." Counts Montholon and Marchand both expressed their surprise at the discovery † I had made, and said they had not known of such a card being within the box, but Count Montholon added he had been charged to present the box to your Ladyship. The other gold box which had the N cut upon the top of it, Count Montholon told me he had been directed to present to Dr. Arnott. It was half full of snuff, being the last box Bonaparte had in use, and the N upon it had been cut by himself. He had directed also a "somme d'argent" to be delivered to Dr. Arnott. I have acquainted Lord Bathurst of these bequests.

"Praying my best respects to Lord Holland, I remain,

"Your Ladyship's most obliged

"and most faithful Servant,

(Signed) "H. Lowe."

* It should be VI.

† I am not sure that Sir Hudson Lowe did not mean to imply by this expression that but for his *discovery* the box would never have reached its destination. At least, observations of his nearly to that purport have been repeated to me. But the legacy is bequeathed and described in the will. Indeed it is the first, or nearly the first article in it. Any insinuation of a wish or a design any where to defraud Lady Holland of the box would be as groundless as it would be malicious.

The legacy announced in the preceeding letter, and which was some months afterward delivered in great form* to Lady Holland at Holland House by the Counts Montholon and Bertrand, was mentioned in the public newspapers very soon after the intelligence of the death of Napoleon had reached Paris. That circumstance and the notoriety of the attention shown by Lady Holland to the illustrious prisoner during his exile, introduced us to the society of those who openly professed or sincerely felt most veneration for the memory of Napoleon in France. From their conversation the substance of the following notes is derived; but as the reader may be desirous to know how far I was qualified either to correct or estimate the representations I heard, by any previous personal observation, it may be necessary to state the extent and nature of such little intercourse as subsisted between Napoleon and us, either before or after his captivity.

Both Lady Holland and myself were presented to him in 1802, when he was First Consul. He saw her only once, and addressed some usual questions and compliments to her, but had no conversation; though I have reason to believe that he was aware of the admiration she entertained and avowed for his military and political genius. I stood next to him in the circle when he received and answered, in a short written speech (hastily and somewhat awkwardly delivered), the deputation head-

* The two gentlemen came in the Imperial uniform! Strange and mortifying reflection to human pride that those who had devoted themselves to a man of great intellect, should imagine that they honored his memory by aping the absurd forms of other sovereigns or pretenders.

ed by Barthelemi, which came to confer upon him the consulship for life. He spoke very civilly, but very little to me on that occasion; and scarcely more when I dined and passed the evening at his court, in company with Mr. Fox, with whom he conversed at considerable length on various matters, and more particularly on the Concordat. These were the only opportunities I ever had of observing his countenance or hearing his voice. The former, though composed of regular features, and both penetrating and good-humored, was neither so dignified nor so animated as I had expected; but the latter was sweet, spirited, and persuasive in the highest degree, and gave a favorable impression of his disposition as well as of his understanding. His manner was neither affected nor assuming, but certainly wanted that ease and attraction which the early habits of good company are supposed exclusively to confer. We traveled through France to Spain that year (1802), and received from the prefects and public officers of every town we passed through, every possible mark of attention. We attributed this to its real cause, the disposition of the Consul to cultivate the good-will of the friends of peace in England, and of all connections of Mr. Fox in particular, and my old friendship with Talleyrand, who was at that time his confidential minister, and not disinclined to give full effect to the general policy of the Consular government in the shape of particular acts of kindness and judicious hospitality to us.

After the first abdication, and the retreat of the Emperor to Elba in 1814, Lady Holland conveyed from Florence and from Rome some messages of civility, and furnished him with one or two packets of English newspapers, which she was informed he had been anxious to peruse, and unable to procure. In acknowledgement of these little acts of attention, I think that he sent her, before he left Elba, some small but curious specimens of the iron ore of that island. It is remarkable that in one of those papers so sent by Lady Holland, was a paragraph hinting a project among the confederates of transporting him to St. Helena. True it is, that such an idea, however inconsistent with honor or good faith, was started and discussed,* though probably never committed to paper at the Congress of Vienna, before Napoleon left Elba. It is just to add, that it was discountenanced and rejected by Austria. In confirmation of so base a design having been entertained, it is observable that a negotiation with the East India Company to place St. Helena† under the control of Government, with no other probable or ostensible object for such a measure, was actually commenced in March, 1815, and discontinued on the landing of Napoleon in that month. Any well-grounded suspicion of such a proceeding was surely sufficient to release the exiled Emperor from the obligations of his treaty and abdication of Fontainebleau, and to justify his attempt to recover the Empire he had so recently lost. We were at Rome

* I stated this fact in the House of Lords in the debate on the treatment of General Bonaparte, and *I was not contradicted:* I had it in truth from an Englishman of veracity employed at the Congress of Vienna, who told it me after Napoleon's arrival at Paris, but before the battle of Waterloo.

† From Admiral Fleming, nephew of the East Indian Director Elphinston, both men of honor, veracity, and intelligence.

when he reached Paris, and at the suggestion, I believe, of his brother Louis, he sent us a passport, which reached us on our journey between Radicofani and Sienna. We never endeavored to avail ourselves of it. The rapid termination of the war rendered it unnecessary. If we had, we should, in all likelihood, have found it useless, for the jealousy of the allies had rigorously closed all communication or intercourse whatever with France. We arrived at Dover nearly at the same time that Napoleon was brought to England in the Bellerophon by Captain Frederick Maitland. That high-spirited officer's scruples in promising nothing but what he knew he could perform, his steadfast adherence to what he did promise, and his conduct throughout both to his illustrious prisoner and his own government, were highly honorable to the character of the service and himself; but generosity to a fallen enemy, neither in his case nor in that of Captain Usher, who had conveyed Napoleon to Elba, recommended those who displayed it to the favor of the Admiralty. The headstrong zeal of Napoleon's adherents has often injured his cause, and exposed him to the imputation of indirectness and perfidy, which he sometimes but very rarely deserved. Some of them most injudiciously as well as falsely accused Captain Maitland of artifice in inveigling the Emperor on board, and of equivocation in interpreting the conditions on which he received him. To neither of these most unfounded charges was Napoleon himself directly or indirectly a party; and the falsehood contained in them, as well as in many other writings of his eager partisans, can not in equity reflect on his personal or political character.

When the ungenerous decision* by which this great prisoner was to be conveyed to St. Helena was known, Lady Holland hastened to apply to government for permission to send such articles as in her judgment were likely to contribute to his comfort or amusement in that distant exile. She improved her slight acquaintance with Sir Hudson Lowe, and by every civility in her power endeavored to obtain from him all the facilities consistent with his duty and instructions for carrying her intentions into execution. She failed in both these attempts. Lord Bathurst informed her that no present could be sent to General Bonaparte, but that government would willingly purchase and convey to him any thing which could be suggested as conducive to his comfort. Lady Holland happened to know that the Emperor liked even in less sultry climates to drink both water and wine extremely cold. She had been on the point of buying, at a considerable price, a newly invented machine for making ice; and in answer to Lord Bathurst's message, she gave him the direction of the maker, and suggested the purchase. The machine, however, was neither purchased nor sent. Lady Holland nevertheless persisted, and contrived to send

* With whom that decision originated, I am not sure. Nothing could be less liberal or dignified than the subsequent conduct and language of George IV. respecting Napoleon and his family. It was a contrast, not a copy, of the Black Prince to King John. Yet the first impression produced on his mind by Napoleon's celebrated letter, if not very creditable to the taste or judgment of the Prince Regent, was not unfavorable to the writer. He remarked that the words with which it began, "Altesse Royale," were quite correct and proper, "more correct, I must say," added he, "than any I ever received from Louis XVIII."

together with new publications and trifling presents to Sir Hudson, similar marks of remembrance to Napoleon. They were often delayed, from excessive scruple or from less pardonable motives, at the Government House; yet the innocent nature of the memorials themselves secured their ultimately reaching their destination. Various obstacles however, presented themselves to this insignificant intercourse. A natural and pardonable pride deterred Napoleon from applying for any thing; a more mistaken, and in my judgment contemptible punctilio, led him to reject any communication in which his title of Emperor was not preserved. Advantage was taken of such circumstances to withhold many convenient and necessary supplies, and to straiten his intercourse with the inhabitants of the island, or with such strangers as accidentally visited it. The privations and petty vexations to which the inhabitants of Longwood were exposed, are probably misrepresented or exaggerated by the vulgarity and ignorance of the author, in the publication of Santini in 1817; but there was undeniably a shameful want of attention to their wishes and interests, and occasionally unmannerly harshness in the Governor toward the illustrious prisoner and his companions. There was little or no tenderness to his feelings, or to those of his family, in the Secretary of State's office at home. If letters from his relations were not actually intercepted, no facility was afforded for conveying them. One from his mother was not only read but mislaid for a considerable time among the inferior clerks of the office. As Napoleon prudently declined drawing on the funds he possessed in Europe, because the drafts and consequently the depositaries of such sums must have been in that case communicated to his jailers and enemies, and as much required by himself and his suite was *not* furnished to them by the English Government, he was compelled to borrow from the private fortunes of his companions, or to raise money in the island by the sale of his plate and other superfluities. The notoriety of such circumstances, possibly the sensation excited by the publication above alluded to, and the effect, I flatter myself, of my motion* in the House of Lords, produced some little relaxation. At least letters from the Emperor's family intrusted to the Secretary of State were henceforward more regularly transmitted. Provisions, clothing, and books purchased by them and sent to the same office, were also forwarded; and Lord Bathurst, some time afterward, not only consented to convey articles from Lady Holland to Napoleon and Sir Hudson Lowe, but apprised her regularly of ships that sailed for St. Helena, and after due experience of her scrupulous adherence to the rules he imposed, allowed all parcels, books, and cases indorsed with her handwriting and name to proceed without further inspection to their destination. Lady Holland had the satisfaction of knowing that many of those articles were received and approved of. Napoleon never wrote, but he mentioned her name and her attentions more than once to persons who repeated his acknowledgments to her. The legacy was, however, a gratifying, and by her an unex-

* The motion referred to some facts in common with the statement of Santini, but it was in nowise connected with that pamphlet or its author, nor did the information on which I grounded it rest in any degree on his authority and representations, as Lord Bathurst in his answer, with some dexterity, affected to think it did.

pected proof, that such endeavors to express her admiration of his great qualities, and even to soothe his afflictions had not been altogether unsuccessful. The testimony of his own handwriting, the words so judiciously chosen, even the pains taken to fit the card to the box, enhanced the value of the bequest, for they proved that Napoleon understood her motives, and that they had occupied for some little space of time the thoughts, as well as excited the good-will of that extraordinary man. The whole was in good taste. Had the gift been greater, she could not have accepted it; had the expressions been stronger, they would not have appeared sincere. Surely to have afforded satisfaction to a man so calumniated, so persecuted, and so ill-treated, and to have excited the esteem of a mind so capacious and so penetrating, is no slight distinction. Lady Holland found in the knowledge of it an ample reward for her constant, unremitting, and unostentatious compassion and generosity. There was a disposition in the people of Paris to disbelieve in the death of Napoleon, there was more in the middling classes to attribute it to poison, and there was some in the court to affect the magnanimity of stifling all resentment toward the departed hero.

> " Cæsar could weep, the crocodile could weep,
> To see his rival of the universe
> Lie still and peaceful there."

It was easier to imitate the hypocrisy than the other qualities of a Cæsar.*

Mourning was worn by many, especially on the 15th August, the festival of St. Napoleon. Publications on his

* See the documents in Appendix V.

character, life, and death were numerous, and generally more full of commendation than of censure. Portraits, engravings, and prints in allusion to his exile and death were bought up with an avidity which alarmed the police, and led to a temporary suppression of the exhibition of such articles in the shops.

The substance of the conversation of those best informed on such subjects in Paris, 1821, may be collected from the following notes of what I heard; I do not vouch for the correctness of every particular. Where, however, I do not mention the relater, I consider the source from which I derive the facts to be authentic, or I have heard them so frequently asserted without contradiction, that I believe them. Where I do mention the relater, the reader may judge of the value of the evidence I adduce.

Enough is known, from his own testimony or others' researches, to satisfy the curiosity of the public about his descent, and to prove, in refutation of the vulgar calumnies of the day, that if neither illustrious nor extraordinary, it was such as, according to the usual way of estimating such matters in France and Italy, would entitle his family to the appellation of noble.* His father was on some occasion chosen as deputy of that class, and both he and one of his sisters were educated at schools in France, where proofs of their belonging to a gentleman's family were exacted. By the concurrent testimony of more than one of his relations, his uncle Ramolino,† a Canon of

* Serra, Pozzo di Borgo, Louis Bonaparte, Napoleon's own conversations, and many other persons as well as documents confirm this fact.

† Pozzo di Borgo thought, when I related this circumstance to him, which I had heard from Fesch and Louis Bonaparte, that it must

Ajaccio, was a man remarkable for his sense and attainments, and of sagacity sufficient to discern the superiority of his nephew, and to recommend on his death-bed all the young men of the family to defer in the most important concerns of their lives to the judgment and advice of their second brother, Napoleon.

Napoleon was born at Ajaccio in 1769. It was affirmed by many that he was at least a year older, and concealed his real age from an unwillingness to acknowledge his birth in Corsica, at a period when that island formed no part of the French dominions. The story is an idle one. A yet more idle one was circulated that he had been baptized by the name of Nicholas,* but from apprehension of

have been his paternal uncle, Lucien Bonaparte, not his maternal uncle Ramolino, of whom it was related. I think I read in the MS. memoirs of Louis Bonaparte which he lent me at Rome in 1815, but which I must allow were almost illegible from the badness of the writing, all that is here related in the text.

* It is said, probably with as little foundation, that when Marshal Soult wished to be proclaimed King of Portugal, his name of Nicholas was urged as an unsurmountable objection. I do not vouch for his having ever entertained such a wish, am satisfied no such objection defeated it, and believe his name to be John. General Sebastiani told me in conversation a curious anecdote about this general, King Joseph, and Napoleon. The latter, when at Madrid, signed a decree annexing Spain to France, and Sebastiani found King Joseph, to whom it had been communicated, in despair, and actually in tears: he earnestly entreated Sebastiani to go to his brother and intercede with him. Napoleon said it was true the decree had been signed, but the news from Salamanca (where I think the English had advanced upon Soult) had induced the Emperor to *revoke the decree*, and to postpone his brother's dethronement for some months. "You may tell him the revocation of the decree (said he), but not a word of my future inten-

ridicule converted it, when he rose to celebrity, into Napoleon. The printed exercises of the military school of Brienne,* of the years **1780, 1781, 1783,** preserved in the Bibliothèque at Paris, represent him as proficient in history, algebra, geography, and dancing, under the name of Buona-Parte de l'Isle de Corse; sometimes d'Ajaccio en Corse. Many traits of his aspiring and ambitious character, even in early youth, have been related, and Pozzo di Borgo quoted (1826) a conversation with him when 18 years of age, in which, after inquiring and learning the state of Italy, he exclaimed, "Then I have not been deceived, and with two thousand soldiers a man might make himself king (Principe) of that country." The ascendency he acquired over his family and companions, long before his great talents had emerged from obscurity, were formerly described to me by Cardinal

tions." Sebastiani some months afterward commanded at Grenada; and he was sounded by a confidential agent of Joseph's and *Soult's* to co-operate in opening a negotiation for a separate peace between Spain and England, unknown to Napoleon and the French government. So that the Imperial councils were far from being a scene of harmony and union at that period.

* These books are as follows:

That of 1780, in which he is twice mentioned; printed at *Troyes*, and unbound.

That of 1781, in which he is mentioned three times; printed by Didot l'ainé, à Paris, and bound.

That of 1782, in which he is mentioned three times; printed at Troyes, and unbound.

N.B. They were all three lent to me in February, 1826, from the Bibliothèque Royale. His name is uniformly written Buona-Parte. He is once described as d'*Ajaccio en Corse*, and twice de *l'Isle de Corse*.

Fesch and Louis Bonaparte, and have been confirmed since by the uniform testimony of such as knew him during his residence in Corsica, or before his acquaintance with Barras, the Director. When at home he was extremely studious, ardent in some pursuit, either literary or scientific, which he communicated to no one. At his meals, which he devoured rapidly, he was silent, and apparently absorbed in his own thoughts. Yet he was generally consulted on all questions affecting the interests of any branch of his family, and on all such occasions was attentive, friendly, decisive, and judicious. He wrote at a very early period of his life a History of Corsica, and sent the manuscript to the Abbé Raynal with a flourishing letter, soliciting the honor of his acquaintance, and requesting his opinion of the work. The Abbé acknowledged the letter and praised the performance, but Napoleon never printed it.* Persons who have dined with him at taverns and coffee-houses when it was convenient to him not to pay his reckoning, have assured me, that though the youngest and poorest, he always obtained, without exacting it, a sort of deference or even submission from the rest of the company. Though never parsimonious, he was at that period of his life extremely attentive to the details of expense, the price of provisions, and of other necessary articles, and in short to every branch of domestic economy. The knowledge thus early acquired in such matters was useful to him in a more exalted station. He cultivated and even made a parade of his information in subsequent periods of his career, and thus

* See Appendix No. VI.

sometimes detected and frequently prevented embezzlement in the administration of public accounts. Nothing could exceed the order and regularity with which his household, both as Consul and Emperor, was conducted. The great things he accomplished, and the savings he made, without even the imputation of avarice or meanness, with the sum comparatively inconsiderable of 15 millions of francs a year, are marvelous, and expose his successors, and indeed all European Princes to the reproach of negligence or incapacity. In this branch of his government, he owed much to Duroc. It is said, that they often visited the markets of Paris (les halles) dressed in plain clothes, and early in the morning. When any great accounts were to be submitted to the Emperor, Duroc would apprise him in secret of some of the minuteest details. By an adroit allusion to them, or a careless remark on the points upon which he had received such recent and accurate information, Napoleon contrived to impress his audience with a notion that the master's eye was every where. For instance, when the Tuilleries were furnished, the upholsterer's charges, though not very exorbitant, were suspected by the Emperor to be higher than the usual profit of that trade would have warranted. He suddenly asked some minister who was with him how much the egg at the end of the bell-rope should cost? "J'ignore," was the answer.—"Eh bien! nous verrons," said he, and then cut off the ivory handle, called for a valet, and bidding him dress himself in plain and ordinary clothes, and neither divulge his immediate commission or general employment to any living soul, directed him to inquire the price of such articles at several shops in Paris, and to order a dozen as for himself. They were one-third less dear than those furnished to the palace. The Emperor, inferring that the same advantage had been taken in the other articles, struck a third off the whole charge, and directed the tradesman to be informed that it was done at his express command, because on *inspection* he had himself discovered the charges to be by one-third too exorbitant. When afterward, in the height of his glory, he visited Caen with the Empress Maria Louisa and a train of crowned heads and princes, his old friend M. Mechin, the Prefect, aware of his taste for detail, waited upon him with five statistical tables of the expenditure, revenue, prices, produce, and commerce of the department. "C'est bon," said he, when he received them the evening of his arrival, "vous et moi nous ferons bien de l'esprit sur tout cela demain au Conseil." Accordingly, he astonished all the leading proprietors of the department at the meeting next day, by his minute knowledge of the prices of good and bad cider, and of the produce and other circumstances of the various districts of the department. Even the Royalist gentry were impressed with a respect for his person, which gratitude for the restitution of their lands had failed to inspire, and which, it must be acknowledged, the first faint hope of vengeance against their enemies entirely obliterated in almost every member of that intolerant faction.

Other princes have shown an equal fondness for minute details with Napoleon, but here is the difference. The use they made of their knowledge was to torment their inferiors and weary their company: the purpose to which Napoleon applied it was to confine the expenses of the

State to the objects and interests of the community. I return to the earlier period of his life. His compliances with the ruling party of the Jacobins have been greatly exaggerated. Some indecorous language and behavior in the churches of Toulon or Marseilles, after the surrender of those towns to the Republicans, constitute the amount of the charges which can be substantiated against him on that score. From all participation in their cruelties he was entirely free. He did not even at that dangerous period conceal from his intimates his contempt for the prevalent absurdities, and his serious disapprobation of the means by which the system of terror was so long kept in vigor. The horrors of the revolution made a deep impression on his mind. The dread of their revival led him at subsequent periods of his life, not only to treat the anti-revolutionists with improvident and dangerous indulgence, but even to assimilate his own government in too many particulars to the ancient order of things. He was apt to listen with complacency to any reasoning which could be devised to ground his authority on a basis the very reverse of that on which he well knew it really, or at least more naturally rested. His favor with Barras (which I believe is correctly stated by all his biographers to have been the chief cause of his employment on the 13th and 14th of Vendemiaire (4th and 5th October, 1795), and his subsequent appointment to the command of the army of Italy) was the fair fruits of his distinguished services at Toulon, and of the genius and energy which, on intimate acquaintance with him, were discernible in his conversation and character. On his first nomination to the army of Italy, the Directory is said to have been unable or unwilling to supply him with the money necessary for the journey of himself and his aid-de-camps to the spot, and their suitable appearance at the head-quarters of a considerable force. In this emergency, after collecting all that his resources, the contribution of his friends, and his credit could muster, he is reported to have applied to Junot, a young officer whom he knew to be in the habit of frequenting the gaming tables, and confiding to him all the money he had been able to raise, in itself no great sum,* to have directed him either to lose the whole or to increase it to a considerable amount before the morning, as on his success that night at play depended the possibility of his taking the command of the army and appointing Junot his aid-de-camp. Junot, after succeeding beyond his expectations in winning to an amount in his judgment equal to the exigencies of his employer, hastened to inform General Bonaparte, but he was not satisfied, and resolving to try his fortune to the utmost, bade his friend return, risk all that he had gained, and not quit the table till he had lost the last penny, or doubled the sum he had brought back to him. In this also, after some fluctuation, the chances favored him, and Napoleon set out to his head-quarters furnished with sufficient to take upon him the command with no little personal splendor and éclat.† The above anecdote

* Junot, say others, sold his silver-hilted sword, and added the produce to the stake.

† I have repeated it as, after refreshing my memory by references to others who heard it at the same time, I believe it to have been told to me. I do not venture to mention the sums, but what was ultimately won, seems to me to have been 300,000 francs. The story,

was first related to me by the Chevalier Serra, Minister of the Ligurian Republic at Madrid, a man of veracity, learning, and discernment; who was intimately acquainted with Napoleon during his Italian campaigns. By the same authority I was assured that at that early period of his career, though he acknowledged the military prowess of the French, he spoke of them to Salicetti and other Italians as foreigners, undervalued their political talents, and treated them as a nation devoid of public principle and moral courage. It is to be remarked that this language was held to Italians, who he well knew would be pleased and flattered by the expression of opinions congenial with their own, and from which they might infer the superiority of their own countrymen over those who in appearance had subdued them. He had married Josephine, the widow of Viscount Beauharnois before he took the command of the army of Italy. During his love for that lady, General Hoche was there, as elsewhere, his rival. Hoche had the advantage of person, higher rank, and a longer established reputation in the army. Josephine with good manners, some beauty, and more sweetness of disposition, had some tincture of romance and superstition in her character. Half in joke, and half in earnest, she was a great promoter of that spurious offspring of astrology and witchcraft which consists in telling fortunes by games of cards, caballistic

with some variation of circumstances, has often been recounted to me, or alluded to in conversation with well-informed Frenchmen. Serra was afterward employed in a diplomatic character by Napoleon at Dresden. He wrote and printed an account of that great prince's German and Polish campaigns in Latin, and died at Dresden in 1813.

numbers, lotteries, palmistry, and other devices, which those who encourage them are compelled to laugh at and term mere pastime, but which those who laugh at them and find diversion in them are apt in some little measure to consider, and even to credit. Napoleon, to amuse his mistress and torment his rival, affected to be an adept in palmistry. He told the fortunes of most of the company in a way which, never having been mentioned since, turned out probably ill-founded conjecture, but on inspecting the hand of Hoche he predicted that his rival would deprive him of his mistress, and that he would die in his bed. As both these events occurred, the credulous and malignant enemies of Napoleon did not fail to impute the second as well as the first to his machinations. The premature death of the young and brilliant General Hoche in Germany was gravely accounted for by poison administered to him by his successful rival in Italy, who forsooth, to avoid suspicion and detection, had in a moment of gayety unnecessarily predicted the death he was secretly and wickedly contriving!

Among the various fortunes foretold to Josephine before her second marriage, she often mentioned that of a gipsy, who had informed her that "she would be greater than a queen, and yet die in a hospital." The latter part of that silly prophecy, say the credulous, has been verified to the letter, though not in the spirit, by the name of *Malmaison*, the place of her decease, which in its original meaning, and probably destination, was a receptacle for the sick. I must acknowledge that I heard the prediction very currently reported as early as 1802, and, therefore, before her death or elevation to the title of Empress, when it might have been matter of dispute whether, as wife of the First Consul, she had literally fulfilled even the first clause of the oracle. His marriage was the work of Barras, and contracted about the time of his promotion. Napoleon's love for Josephine was ardent and sincere; it continued for some time, and his esteem and good-will toward her never ceased. Upon first assuming the title of Emperor, he began, however, to listen to suggestions, and, perhaps, to harbor the design of another marriage, calculated to insure his admittance into the college of legitimate sovereigns, and better suited to the foundation of an hereditary empire, by affording some prospect of issue. A lady who knew Josephine well, but who, though correct in her recollections and accurate in her language, is apt somewhat to dramatize her narratives, assured me that, on first assuming his new title, the Emperor told Madame Bonaparte in her cabinet that his family, his ministers, his council, *enfin tout le monde*, had represented to him the necessity of a divorce and a new marriage; and that while she was leaning on her arm, with tears in her eyes, he walked backward and forward in a hurried and agitated manner, frequently repeating, "Qu'en dis-tu donc? Cela sera-t-il? Qu'en dis-tu?" She replied, "Que veux-tu que j'en dise? Si tes frères, tes ministres, tout le monde est contre moi, et il n'y a que toi pour me défendre!" "Tu n'as que moi pour te défendre!" exclaimed he with emotion, "Eh bien, tu l'emporteras." Josephine, in recounting the story, added that he never could withstand tears, and least of all the tears of a woman. According to her, whenever he thought it necessary to be firm, he assumed a short, harsh, and decisive tone, for the purpose of preventing those ap peals which he was unable directly to resist. Others have concurred in assuring me that the unmannerly speeches in which he too often indulged were the result of system rather than temper, and adopted to disconcert designs and elude importunity; that his so much dreaded bursts of passion were the cloak of an easy and good-humored, not the ebullitions of a hasty or ungovernable disposition. This may be so; but many will think he acted his part too well, and habit too often becomes second nature.

On one melancholy occasion he certainly exhibited great obduracy. Whatever were the motives, whoever were the advisers of the arrest and execution of the Duke of Enghien, Napoleon was besieged both in public and private by the tears of his wife, the intercession of his family, and the remonstrances of more than one public man, for mercy, and in vain. The whole is a mystery; those who were in the secret, and have written on the subject, without succeeding in vindicating themselves from all suspicion of participation in the guilt, have thrown little light on the subject. One of them, Savary, had at one time committed to paper the following explanation of the motives for arresting the Duke of Enghien.* Those intrusted with the

* The manuscript of his memoirs containing this story, was offered for sale to a bookseller in London in 1815 or 1816, by Savary himself. The bookseller, to form a judgment of its value, confided it to the perusal of Mr. Allen, who, though he abstained, from a scruple of honor, from copying a line, recollected the account of this interesting and painful transaction. The memoir was neither purchased by the bookseller nor printed, and in the pamphlet afterward published by Savary, in Paris, some of the details were repeated verbatim, others were altered, and others entirely suppressed.

police had information of the private meetings of Georges Cadoudal and his accomplices at Paris. Their numbers, their plot, the means they possessed of executing it, and the period destined for their enterprise, even much of their private conversation, had been detected. But in those secret juntos there occasionally appeared a person whose name and character were never accurately ascertained. He was treated with marks of unusual outward respect, and seemed to be considered among the Royalist assassins to be a personage of great rank and importance. Though he afterward turned out to have been Pichegru, he was conjectured by the Chief Consul and his government to be no other than the Duke of Enghien. That Prince was known to have been recently hovering on the confines of Germany and France, and to have absented himself somewhat mysteriously from his usual residence in the former country for a fortnight, during which time the appearance of the distinguished conspirator at Paris had occurred. The orders for his seizure were accordingly issued under the persuasion that he was the man. Supposing the story to be true, the motives for the execution of that unfortunate Prince, once brought to Paris, even though the mistake were cleared up, would be more intelligible, though perhaps not much more excusable than a wanton outrage of neutral territory for the purpose of seizing an innocent and interesting young man. Such a view of the transaction would be consistent with a speech imputed by Napoleon, in his conversation with Lord Elvington, to Talleyrand. "Le vin est tiré, il faut le boire." His regret, too, at not having seen the Duke, and the inference he left to be drawn that, had he seen him, *he must have pardoned him,* would tally well with this explanation of the transaction.* On the other hand, is it probable that Napoleon, aware of the reproaches to which this incident of his life had exposed him, and not averse to hear or even to discuss the sensation it had produced, should never, either at Elba, or at Paris during the 100 days, on the voyage, or at St. Helena, have urged such circumstances in palliation of the judicial murder, which, unless some false impression on his mind at the time can be proved, or some unknown provocation be adduced, he must be allowed to have perpetrated? A crime is not to be palliated, much less to be justified by its consequences. What though the terror inspired by the death of a Bourbon Prince enabled Napoleon to spare many conspirators of that party, who had forfeited their lives to the law—what though he availed himself largely of that power, exhibiting in the case of the Polignacs, the Marquis de Rivière, and many others, a clemency almost unexampled in any government similarly circumstanced, still the unprovoked sacrifice of a man whom position and birth alone made an enemy, and against whom no crime was even alleged, will and ought to remain a blot upon his memory. Future disclosures may soften the dye, but none that I can conjecture can entirely efface the stain which that guilt has left on his government. It is just to add that having read the official orders and correspondence relating to the seizure

* Our Edward I. refused an interview with David, Prince of Wales, when resolved to execute him. James II. saw Monmouth, and had the heart to refuse a pardon. I believe Napoleon, like Edward, thought an interview and pardon almost synonymous, and condemnation of an equal with whom he had recently conversed not only severity but brutality.

of the Duke of Enghien, I am satisfied that Caulincourt, Duke of Vicence, had no participation in the guilt, and very remotely any, if indeed he had any, in the measures for seizing that unfortunate Prince. The orders were given from Paris through the regular channels. Berthier wrote and forwarded the military instructions; Talleyrand, as Minister of Foreign Affairs, the justification of that breach of neutrality. General Ordener, *not* General Caulincourt, received those orders; an inferior officer of the name of Charlotte, under the immediate orders of the same General Ordener, and *not* of General Caulincourt, executed them. I presume that, had Caulincourt, or any other general on service, received such orders, he would have executed them without scruple. The civil, and not the military authorities, if the latter act under orders, are, both in law and sense, alone responsible for such infraction of neutrality. But, in this instance, General Caulincourt was not the military authority who received the orders or executed them. It is equally clear from undeniable documents, that he was at Nancy, a distance too great from Paris to communicate with the government in the interval between the arrival of the Duke of Enghien and his execution. He could, therefore, have had no influence on the fate of the Prince. His friends assert that he would have exerted any he had in his favor; and they add, that on his arrival at Paris, two days afterward, he fainted away at the recital of his death; a degree of emotion, it must be acknowledged, somewhat unaccountable in a person so utterly unconnected with the victim, and so very remotely and innocently, if at all, implicated in any part of the transaction. His solicitation to be employed in it, his journey to Strasburgh for that purpose, his presence at the court-martial and execution, together with many imputations on his character, are manifestly the invention of libelists. His relations assure me that the dependence of his father or family on the late Prince of Condé, so confidently reported, and so vehemently urged in aggravation of his supposed guilt, is equally void of foundation. Napoleon, in the 100 days, when apprised on inquiry that the grounds of the enmity felt toward Caulincourt by the Bourbon princes was his supposed participation in the arrest and execution of their relation, observed to Count Molé—"Mais il n'a rien eu a y faire, pas plus que vous."

On the first breaking out of the war in 1803, Napoleon had some design of changing his title and assuming the crown. He had indeed been inclined to do so before, but had been prevented by his generals, and especially by Lannes.* He in truth always treated the latter with great forbearance and affection, allowed him to cross his designs, and even overlooked his deviations from important duties. This conduct arose from a grateful recollection of his early services, and from an unvarying, perhaps a systematic predilection for all his first military comrades and connections. The epithets of ungrateful and vindictive seem necessary appendages to the titles of usurper and tyrant, which were so liberally conferred on our formidable enemy by the English. Yet successful

* Afterward Duke of Monte Bello, and always a generous, frank, gallant, and fearless soldier, with strong republican predilections, and liable to no reproaches, but such as a disregard of decorum and indelicacy on subjects relating to public money exposed him to.

ambition has rarely been so free from the reproach of ingratitude or revenge as in the instance of Napoleon.

He made the treaty of Amiens as an experiment, and the scurrility of our newspapers, the coldness, jealousy, and obvious estrangement of our cabinet, convinced him that the experiment had failed. He employed one of the best pens in France, M. Gallois, to draw up the report on the peace of Amiens, in which the articles were justified, and the advantages of the peace earnestly impressed on the legislature. When Lord Whitworth left Paris on the rupture, Napoleon sent again for Gallois and exclaimed, "Eh bien! l'Angleterre veut absolument la guerre. Elle la veut." He then laid before M. Gallois the whole negotiation, and pressed him to give his opinion. "England," said Gallois, "might have done more to preserve peace, but France has not done all she might to obtain it." To that remark, the Chief Consul answered that he had already dispatched another messenger to catch Lord Whitworth, and "de faire cette dernière tentative.* But after vaunting and proving his efforts for peace, and after acknowledging that peace, or at least the utmost endeavors to preserve it had been necessary for France, he added with emphasis but with gayety: "Mais enfin, je vous dis, l'Angleterre veut la guerre. Elle l'aura, at quant à moi, j'en suis ravi.† Pressed to explain a feel-

* This was to leave England in possession of Malta, but to stipulate that she should employ her mediation with the King of Sicily for the cession of Tarento, Otranto, and one other port to France. A Genevan, named Hubert, was the bearer of this ultimatum. It was rejected.

† The precise sentiment expressed in other language by Mr. Pitt in his speech on the rupture of the negotiations at Lisle. The coin cidence is curious.

ing apparently so inconsistent with his professions, he entered into a long, curious, and luminous exposition of his policy. "If," said he, "the Powers of Europe had been willing to let France and her new institutions subside into a tranquil and free government, if they could have borne *de bonne foi* to cultivate the relations of amity with her and her dependencies in Holland and Italy, she might have cherished the arts of peace, improved her internal condition, and sat down contented with the prospects of liberty and prosperity before her; but experience of peace for one year with England, and for more with the other powers, has confirmed my apprehensions and proved it to be hopeless. They never meant to leave France unmolested. But France who would be hereafter unequal, is just now fully equal to contend with them all to advantage." "How so," said M. Gallois; "will not some years of peace add to the resources of France? Will not the beneficial effects of those changes, of which we have hitherto perceived little but the shock, be gradually sensible in the increasing riches and power of this great people?" "Granted," replied Bonaparte, "but riches and prosperity, for the purposes I am contemplating, may not be altogether the instruments best adapted to the end: d'ailleurs, l'armée! les généraux!" He described the latter at that moment, flushed with success, inured to fatigue, with fortunes half made, in all the vigor of life, and ardor of aspiring ambition. A few years' repose, during which they must be courted and enriched by the government, would damp their ardor and impair their capacity for war, and yet leave them, their descendants, representatives, or favorites, with pretensions to influence and command, difficult and perhaps unjust to elude. In such a state, the country would be unequal to the sort of contest he was then contemplating; for the great powers of the Continent must not merely be humbled—they must be broken, shattered, and dismembered. In their present condition, they had the will, and they would, after a short peace, have the power to combine to wrest from France the fruits of her victories, and, possibly, to blast all her prospects by a counter-revolution.

Napoleon then developed his whole system at great length and in detail. To Gallois it seemed vast and well combined—his views comprehensive, if not just, his argument ingenious and striking, and his knowledge almost miraculous. He pursued the system he then described with little variation, till his marriage with the Archduchess of Austria.

That connection (which, in my humble opinion, degraded him, not her) altered his designs both at home and abroad, tempted him to assimilate his government more and more to other monarchies, and deluded him with the hope that the princes of Europe might, in consideration of his foreign alliances and domestic authority, overlook the faults of his escutcheon, and be reconciled, in the form of an hereditary monarchy, to a title derived from the people. The Empress Josephine very naturally saw, or affected to see, that policy in an opposite light. In addition to her tears and reproaches, she endeavored to deter him from his resolution by predicting that his good fortune would abandon him when he abandoned her; for with their connection, she artfully or superstitiously had always maintained that it was mysteriously interwoven. When he first conceived the design is very difficult to ascertain, especially as all his designs were the offspring of his own inventive mind, and seldom, if ever, suggested to him by others. Talleyrand told me that the Council, and he among them, were strangely embarrassed by the abruptness of the proposal. They were sitting round the table, discussing official matters, when the Emperor suddenly cut them short and said there were three points on which they should deliberate immediately, and decide without any unnecessary loss of time: 1st. Whether it was essential to the interests of the state that he should divorce Josephine for the purpose of insuring succession; 2d. Whether, on so doing, he should marry a princess allied to some ancient dynasty in Europe; 3dly. Whether a Russian or an Austrian would be the most eligible match. To courtiers the question was perplexing. Talleyrand, in recounting it to me, showed, by his countenance, the impression it had made on him at the time. He was not sorry that Cambacères had the precedence of him and was to speak first. By his own acknowledgment he evaded any direct answer, and suggested that the inclinations of the Empress Josephine to lend herself to such a measure, and the means of accomplishing it with or without her consent, should be duly weighed before it was possible to give any answer to the first, much more to the other two questions. But although Talleyrand had not been sounded, others of the Council possibly had been; more than one courtier had discovered that such topics might be canvassed in conversation before and even with Napoleon, without scruple or danger. One strange and obscure man of the name of Nisas pretended that Josephine herself would feel the propriety of some such step, and when reproached by her for giving such advice to the Emperor, openly avowed it, saying, that if she were a good Frenchwoman she would not only submit and contribute to the divorce, but actually urge her husband to accomplish it. It is difficult to believe that any man, however wild, would have ventured to hold such language to the Empress Josephine, unless he had received a hint to do so from Napoleon. The Bonaparte family, either at the suggestion of the Emperor himself, or from jealousy of the Beauharnois (a motive which often swayed their conduct), were active in promoting the design, and maintaining the propriety, justice, and necessity of it. Talleyrand assured me positively, that neither the Emperor Alexander nor the Emperor Francis showed the slightest repugnance to the alliance. The Empress-mother and the Grand Duchess herself were alone averse to it in Russia. Austria in a manner solicited the honor, and one Dumoutier (afterward an ultra-courtier and minister under the Bourbons) was authorized to convey to Napoleon* that his offer would not be unacceptable to the court of Vienna. Both those Imperial cabinets by secret communications at the time, and by subsequent representations, contrived to deceive (no very hard task, I presume) Lord Liverpool and his colleagues, for his Lordship assured me that as to the Archduchess,

"Ne'er was woman in that humor woo'd,
And ne'er was woman in that humor won;"

---

* Or rather to Narbonne, through whom it was communicated to Napoleon.

that it was an assault rather than a courtship, and that if the lady was somewhat less averse to the match than those about her, her father and family bewailed it as a signal misfortune, and that as to the Russian court,* it would never have submitted to the indignity. Napoleon seemed actually in love with Maria Louisa for the first year; he always treated her well, but she was not of a character to inspire much confidence, or of an understanding to afford much resource. She grew, latterly, more tired of the constraint of his court, and he was more reserved and ceremonious, possibly from suspicions of the designs or resentment at the perfidy of the court of Vienna.

How far the previous elevation of Napoleon at various prominent epochs of his eventful career was the result of address and decision at fortunate and critical periods, or the gradual produce and natural fruit of a well-matured foresight and industry, it will be the province of the future biographer and historian to conjecture. That at the peace of Campo-Formio he was aware of the precarious character of the government he *then* served, or rather disobeyed, is clear, from remarks he made to the Austrians, with whom he negotiated. They offered him a retreat, nay, a small principality, in Germany.† He declined it; but in alleging his reasons for so doing, admitted the instability of the Directory, and unsatisfactory state of

* Perhaps as far as the Empress-mother and the Grand Duchess of Oldenburgh (afterward Princess of Wurtemberg) were concerned, this may be true; but it was not true of Alexander or his ministers.

† I had this fact from Murveldt, who negotiated that treaty with him.

France. Indeed, unless convinced of the weakness of the Directory, he would hardly have ventured to disobey their instructions by signing that peace. On his return to Paris, he studied the individuals who composed the Directory and administration. He exposed their foibles with infinite wit, detected their defects, and censured their measures with wonderful sagacity, and little reserve. The society of Paris, which had hitherto contemplated him only as a successful general, perceived that his discernment of character, his quickness of perception, and his comprehensive views of public affairs, qualified him for political command. "Ceci ne peut durer," said he; "ces directeurs ne sçavent *rien faire pour l'imagination de la nation;*" an expression which illustrates not only his contempt of the government then established, but the general view of French character on which he founded much of his subsequent policy. His language was so indiscreet, that the Directory had thoughts of arresting him. Some say they applied to Fouché for that purpose,* and that that wily and profligate man answered; "Ce n'est pas là un homme à arrêter; encore ne suis-je pas l'homme qui l'arrêtera." Whatever be the truth of that anecdote, the jealousy of the Directory did not escape the vigilance of Napoleon. He perceived with some uneasiness that his brilliant victories, his no less brilliant peace, and his popularity in the circles of Paris were insufficient to insure him that ascendency in the army and the government to which he aspired, and that a disclosure of his designs might expose him to danger, notwithstanding all

* Query. Was Fouché Minister of Police before Egypt? [He was appointed July 31st, 1799.]

his services and splendid qualities. From these considerations, though he had granted peace to Austria and to Rome, he became averse to any general pacification, and ardent for employment either in the invasion of England or some other great undertaking. In the mean while, he paid assiduous court to the men of science and literature, attended the Institute constantly, affected to consult the members on matters connected with Government, and to advise or converse with them on those relating to science. All those circumstances contributed to the Egyptian expedition. It was devised partly to get rid of him, partly to gratify him, and partly to dazzle and delight that portion of Parisian society, who through the press and the institutions for education had considerable influence on public opinion. Napoleon also accepted the command from mixed motives, from ambition, from love of glory, and from a consciousness that his indiscreet language had rendered his situation at home somewhat precarious. His good fortune in escaping our fleet under the command of Nelson is well known. His attention to every thing connected with navigation and the management of a ship and a fleet, during the voyage, was remarkable. The army at first landing was disconcerted at the appearance of the country, the towns, villages, and people, and the strange masks of the women. The soldiers and officers were yet more perplexed at the little accommodation for conveyance of themselves or their baggage in their ensuing march, which they were commanded to undertake immediately. The horses were small and few, the camels were not numerous, and even the asses, of which there were abundance, were not fine animals of their sort, but a weak and diminutive as well as ignominious species of cavalry. The indignation against the men of science, who were supposed to be the instigators of the expedition, was loud, and it was at one time apprehended that it might lead to consequences very injurious to their safety. When, however, nothing but asses were allotted to them for their conveyance, their forlorn appearance made them objects of derision rather then anger, and by affording food for the pleasantry of the soldiers, they escaped all serious injury or insult. They and the humble animals they bestrode soon became synonymous terms. "Voila un sçavant," said the soldier when he saw a donkey; and "voici la bête d'âne" when he described a philosopher. Caffarelli, the one-legged general under whose care they were specially placed, and who preceded them seated also on an ass, was occasionally greeted in the same tone: "Le voila," they would say, "il s'en moque bien celui-là; qu'est ce que cela lui fait? il a un pied en France." General Bonaparte connived at, if he did not encourage such jokes, glad to substitute them for more serious murmurs, which he knew the state of his army was but too well calculated to excite.

In the first actions* the detachments of Mamelukes charged the infantry with the greatest confidence. They

* The particulars of the Egyptian expedition which follow, though of no great importance, were related to me in so lively and natural a manner by General Bertrand, on his first return from St. Helena, that I thought them worth preserving; and as Napoleon was, at all periods of his life, especially during his exile, particularly fond of dwelling on all his adventures in Egypt, there is little doubt, but the recollection of General Bertrand had been recently refreshed at St. Helena by conversation on that topic with the Emperor himself.

were utterly astonished at finding themselves repulsed by a compact body of men whom taken separately they despised, not less for their diminutive stature, than for the wretched state of their accoutrements. Murad Bey thought nothing but cowardice could have led to the discomfiture of the first troops he had sent against the invaders. He was near strangling the officer who had commanded them for flying before such "Christian dogs." "As to myself," said he, "I will ride through them and sever their heads from their bodies like water-melons." He did engage them, and at the head of a considerable force, but with no better success. He was thereupon yet more amazed and indignant. So enraged was he, that it was apprehended he would kill himself. When he afterward heard that the French commanders, and especially General Bonaparte and General Desaix, were little men, he imagined the Franch soldiers were fixed together in a machine, and turned by some mechanical contrivance in the centre of each column. He could in no other way account for the steadiness of the phalanx and the regularity of their movements. An interview with General Kleber somewhat consoled him, for General Kleber was tall and handsome. Murad Bey said, on seeing him, that he was glad to find there were at least some *men* in the army with which he had submitted to make a truce. But whatever his impressions or those of other Mamelukes or Egyptians might be on the outward appearance of the French generals, they soon discerned the superiority of Napoleon in moral and intellectual qualities. Some grew to love, others to fear, all to respect him. On suppressing the insurrection of the Cheiks, he executed sixty without delay, and surprised their comrades who came to intercede for them the next morning with the sad intelligence that they had all perished over night. He related this story with an indifference and even with a gayety, to Mr. Fozakerby and others, many years afterward at Elba, which seemed very unfeeling; and though he carelessly observed that he did it to show that *sa manière de gouverner n'étoit pas molle*, he neglected to relate the circumstances which accounted for, and in some sort justified his extraordinary severity to what he called *des abbés de ce pays-là*, nor did he mention the many acts of clemency and of judicious encouragement to the same order of people with which he accompanied and followed that rigorous proceeding. The Cheiks had plotted a massacre of the French soldiers in Cairo. They had actually armed and raised the people in pursuance of that design. The French were exasperated to the highest degree. They had taken sixty Cheiks *flagrante delicto*, but they were with difficulty restrained from sacking the town and murdering such inhabitants as they deemed partisans of the Cheiks. So general in all ranks was such a disposition, that officers of high rank, with Kleber at their head, remonstrated loudly with Napoleon on his supineness, and urged him to punish the natives and extirpate the Cheiks. General Kleber, on finding the chief Cheik, the secret instigator and director of the insurrection, closeted some days afterward with General Bonaparte, was with difficulty prevented from striking and cutting him down with his sabre; he could not refrain from insulting him with opprobrious language mixed with reproaches and menaces. But such was not the policy of

Bonaparte. He, on the contrary, told the old conspirator himself in private, and the body of Cheiks who waited upon him in public, that he was fully aware of their machinations, that he had punished those that were most prominent, and was advised to proceed with the same severity toward those whose guilt (for so of course he called it) was equal and as satisfactorily proved; but he added, he was willing to believe they had repented of their offense, and were aware of the consequences of repeating it; that as they knew he did not fear them, he hoped they would see how much it was their mutual interest to be friends; that he respected their moral qualities and their religion; that from them alone he could learn what were the wants of the people, and through them alone he could hope to administer justice and redress the grievances of the inhabitants. Language so unlike that of their real masters, the Mamelukes, or their pretended sovereigns, the Turks, did not fail to have some effect, especially as it was followed up with actual proofs of confidence, and a certain participation of power in the villages and smaller towns of the country. Napoleon took pains to ingratiate himself with the Cheiks and the Copts, *i.e.*, the mass of the inhabitants, on the following principles. The Mamelukes, even if propitiated, could never, under a French government, be supplied or renovated. However useful their submission or their assistance might be at first, they could give him no permanent hold on the country, and on some nation or caste he clearly foresaw that the French must ultimately lean for the maintenance of their empire in Egypt. He, indeed, and the French government had been misled by their agents into a belief that the Sublime Porte would hail the rescue of Egypt from the Mamelukes as a favor, and might be induced to invest their ancient allies the French, whether Christians or not, with all the authority that the sanction of their distant sovereignty and of their religion could bestow. But such idle hopes were soon dispelled. The inveterate nature of Turkish hostility was soon apparent to Bonaparte, and he was by no means disposed to undervalue their courage or their resources. Their infantry was indeed easily dispersed, and their cavalry far less formidable than that of the Mamelukes; but he was too wise to overlook the advantages which in a protracted contest an enormous empire, the nominal sovereignty of the faithful, and a fearless people at its command, would give the Sublime Porte. The only counterpoise was to be found in the opinions and attachment of the natives. The former depended chiefly on the Cheiks, and the latter was only to be inspired by good treatment and just government. He endeavored, therefore, to improve the condition, to humor the superstitions, and to supply the wants of the Copts, and he strove to court, gratify, and instruct the Cheiks. It is not true that he embraced Islamism, but he complied with many ceremonies, salutations, and usages, and he maintained all the observances exacted by the Cheiks from Frenchmen as well as from Copts. The Porte, the Vizier, or some Turkish authority dispatched more than one assassin to murder him; but the Cheiks, won by his measures, always gave him timely notice of the design, and sometimes secretly and silently, but effectually assisted him in defeating it. In his endeavors to better the condition and improve the industry of the natives, he turned his men of science to some account. He had been anxious on the march to Cairo to provide for their security, and when there he was not inattentive to their comforts. To reconcile them to their hardships and dangers, and to counteract the derision to which they had been exposed, he tickled their vanity, by occasional compliments to their courage as well as their knowledge in his bulletins and dispatches. They were employed in instructing the natives in various arts of life, and superintending the introduction of various inventions and implements, such as windmills, wheelbarrows, hand-saws, etc., with which they had hitherto been unacquainted. Napoleon's departure from Egypt was at the time represented as a desertion of his army, but it is now well known that he had received a letter from his government officially authorizing and practically urging his return to France. When Kleber had succeeded to the command, the Cheiks imagined that the same good-will to them did not prevail at the head-quarters of the French army. They ceased to watch over the safety of the Commander with any solicitude. An emissary of the Turks passed the frontiers, and traveled through the Egyptian villages unmolested. He lurked in the neighborhood of the head-quarters, and having at length succeeded in finding the general separated from his troops, stabbed him to the heart. Officers* who had the best means of forming a judgment have assured me that there was no conspiracy in the country, but they were of opinion that the vigilance of the Cheiks would have protected General Bonaparte from the intrusion of any such assassin.

* Belliard, Sebastiani, Bertrand.

According to the account of Napoleon himself, it was in Egypt that he weaned his mind from all those Republican illusions in which his early growth in fame had been nursed. It is certain that after his elevation to the consulship he seldom if ever betrayed any such propensities. But those who knew him early and well have assured me that the scenes of the Revolution had estranged and even disgusted him with Democracy; that exclusive of that repugnance to all popular interference with authority, which the possession of power breeds, he conscientiously checked every tendency to revive in France, or to produce elsewhere,* any excesses of that nature, from a conviction that the evil created by them is immediate and certain, the ultimate good to be derived from them uncertain and problematical. He knew, indeed, that his glory and power were the offspring of the Revolution. He felt, perhaps he regretted too much, that the enemies of that great change hated "the Child" and supposed "Champion of Jacobinism." He was not even without apprehension that the prosperity and stability of his government, whether called Consular, Regal, or Imperial, would depend on the prevalence of those principles on which great national changes are founded and justified. Yet he was nevertheless disposed to endanger some of his personal security, rather than foment a spirit which he deemed incompatible with tranquil government and a due administration of justice. Like our Elizabeth, his principles and (though not to an equal degree) his temper, too, were at variance with his position. I mention these things in

* In Ireland; in Poland; in Spain.

honor of truth, not of Napoleon. The partisans of authority, of pomp, and perhaps of superstition in government, have a right to the sanction of this great man's opinion, though his endeavors to purchase their assistance were only successful while he stood in no need of it. Much, however, of his conduct toward Royalists and Republicans, Emigrants and Jacobins, especially during his Consulship, sprang from a laudable desire of healing the wounds of the Revolution, and from a sincere, patriotic, and well-suggested design of blending all classes and parties in France, and uniting them in support of a common government and in defense of the country. Soon after his elevation, he began indeed, systematically to disparage the genius of those whose writings were supposed to have produced that alteration of sentiment on politics and religion, which had given direction, if not existence, to the French Revolution. He must in his heart have admired Voltaire. His own manner of seeing many things showed that he had read and studied him too. If not, it proves how the genius and style of that lively yet diligent and profound writer have pervaded the age which succeeds him, and indirectly influence the thoughts and dispositions of the greatest statesmen of our time. I have been confirmed in my conjectures, of the secret admiration of Napoleon for Voltaire, by learning that he frequently read his plays aloud to his little society at St. Helena. He criticised, he censured, he ridiculed, but he read the same play over and over again, and his thoughts were much occupied with the subject. But whether his own satirical turn and quick perception of folly and falsehood were borrowed from Voltaire or not, he certainly was at some pains to decry that great writer's philosophy. He employed Geoffroy and Fontanes to write down the Encyclopedists, and extol the authors of the age of Louis XIV. Under color of vindicating the purity of language, the simplicity of composition, and the classical character of the French drama and poetry, many covert attacks were directed against the political and religious maxims of more recent authors, and yet more undisguised assaults encouraged against the moral character and intellectual attainments of the philosophers. Yet, while under the immediate protection of the Consular and Imperial government this warfare against public opinion was carried on, Napoleon himself, from some private predilection, from remorse, from candor, or from caprice, indulged in some acts of infidelity to his unnatural idols. He liked much, saw frequently, and gave both money and advice to Talma, whose style of acting, adapted to vigorous sallies of passion, and sudden vicissitudes of fortune, seemed connected with the new school, and was accordingly the object of Geoffroy's virulent and incessant abuse. Napoeon procured, if he did not write, some bitter answers to Geoffroy's diatribes on the theatre; and when that servile critic had in his invectives against Voltaire outstripped the bounds of his employer's policy, he secretly atoned for the outrage on departed genius by silently erecting in a church at Paris a marble monument to the great and calumniated Philosopher of Ferney. To Rousseau, he made no such atonement. He always spoke of his works with asperity and contempt, and in one instance took a very ungracious occasion of doing so. "C'etait un mauvais homme, un méchant homme," said he, at Ermenonville, to Stanislas Girardin, who had been educated under the auspices, and whose place was decorated with various monuments in memory of Rousseau. M. Girardin urged the beauty of his style and composition, and palliated the faults of his character by ascribing to him great purity of intention and universal philanthropy. "Non, c'était un méchant homme, *sans lui la France n'auroit pas eu de révolution.*" Girardin, smiling, observed that he was not aware that the First Consul considered the Revolution such an unmixed evil. "Ah!" he exclaimed, "vous voulez dire que sans la révolution vous ne m'auriez pas eu moi? Peut-être pas; je le crois; mais aussi la France n'en serait-elle que plus heureuse." When invited to see the hermitage, the cap, table, great chair, etc., of Jean Jacques, he said, "Ah bah! non, je n'ai aucun gout pour ces niaiseries-là, montrez-les à mon frère Louis; il en est bien digne." He happened, however, to be unusually cross on that day. Josephine had offended him in more ways than one. He was even little enough to be nettled at her sitting down with the rest of the company without waiting for him; for even before he assumed the title of Emperor, he grew somewhat tenacious of outward ceremony, and thought, perhaps, that by exacting it as Consul, he prepared and familiarized men's minds to the etiquette of a court. He was moreover sore at a hint, thrown out half in jest and half in earnest, that his success in shooting had been in consequence of some contrivance to lame the game, or to turn out tame animals, without his knowledge, for him to fire upon. He was a bad shot, but he was above once in his life indignant at discovering such a practice, which he justly remarked was childish and degrading adulation. He was perhaps at all times, and certainly during the first years of his elevation, more liable to unbecoming anger at the abuse and calumnies of the public journals. His irritation at our newspapers contributed to estrange him from England after the Peace of Amiens, and to accelerate and embitter the rupture between the two countries. Yet he was much struck with a remark of M. Gallois, to whom he complained of the licentiousness of the English press. M. Gallois very pertinently observed, that he had volumes and volumes of libel equal in malignity against Louis XIV., but that nothing now was remembered of them but the fretful sensibility which that monarch betrayed about them, and the false steps in policy which more than once they had provoked him to take. Gallois wrote the report on the Peace of Amiens, but he declined composing that on the rupture, which was written by Daru from the same materials as had been furnished to Gallois by the First Consul. Not very long afterward, the name of Gallois was presented in a list for the Legion of Honor; Napoleon unhandsomely erased it, saying with a smile, "Quand on sait bien parler pour la paix, il faut aussi sçavoir bien parler pour la guerre." He continued, however, to converse with Gallois occasionally, in a friendly and even confidential manner; but though favored and even caressed, that independent and modest man observed his growing impatience of contradiction, his propensity to war, and, above all, his determination as well as capacity of governing every thing himself; and he resolved not to place himself in a situation where he could not both with honor and comfort express and follow his own opinion of right or wrong. He therefore declined the prefecture of Besançon, avoided other public employments, and voted silently but uniformly in those assemblies of which he was a member, in favor of that party and those principles which were not hostile to the establishment or revival of any arbitrary power in the state. He ceased to visit the Tuileries, but he never experienced from the Consular or Imperial government, the slightest vexation or persecution. Napoleon, even in the plenitude of his power, seldom gratified his revenge by resorting to any act either illegal or unjust, though he frequently indulged his ill-humor by speaking both of and to those who had displeased him in a manner mortifying to their feelings and their pride. The instances of his love of vengeance are very few: they are generally of an insolent rather than a sanguinary charcter, more discreditable to his head than his heart, and a proof of his want of manners, taste, and possibly feeling, but not of a dye to affect his humanity. Of what man possessed of such extended, yet such disputed authority, can so much be said? Of Washington? of Cromwell? But Washington if he had ever equal provocation and motives for revenge, certainly never possessed such power to gratify it. His glory, greater in truth than that of Cæsar, Cromwell, and Bonaparte, was that he never aspired; but he disdained such power;* he never had it, and can not therefore deserve immoderate praise for not exerting what

* "He might have been a king
But that he understood
How much it was a meaner thing
To be unjustly great than honorably good."
(Verses on Lord Fairfax, by Villiers, Duke of Buckingham.)

he did not possess. In the affair of General Lee, he did not, if I recollect, show much inclination to forgive. Even Cromwell did not possess the power of revenge to the same extent as Napoleon. There is reason, however, to infer from his moderation and forbearance that he would have used it as sparingly. But Cromwell is less irreproachable on the score of another vice, viz., ingratitude. Napoleon not only never forgot a favor, but unlike most ambitious characters never allowed subsequent injuries to cancel his recollection of services. He was uniformly indulgent to the faults of those whom he had once distinguished. He saw them, he sometimes exposed and rectified, but he never punished or revenged them. Many have blamed him for this on the score of policy; but if it was not sense and calculation, it should be ascribed to good-nature. None, I presume, will impute it to weakness or want of discernment. He described himself, however, as a just, not an easy man. "Je ne suis pas *bon*, non, je ne suis pas *bon*, je ne l'ai jamais été, mais je suis *sûr*." True it is, as I have before remarked, that his dislike and even his displeasure seldom led to any persecution, or even permanent exclusion of the objects of it from promotion; though it exposed them to asperity of language and other petty mortifications. He not only preserved in high employment, but advanced to higher, some persons whose opinions were most hostile to his system of government, as well as others of whom he spoke with anger and contempt. In repressing the injustice of all authorities inferior to his own, he was impartial, severe, and inflexible. Neither minister, prefect, officer, nor military authority, could venture to exceed the letter of the law. Never was government, in France at least, so little military as that of Napoleon, never was justice more steadily and equally administered between men, and even between government and its subjects. There was indeed at the latter period of his reign no security whatever against abuse but the knowledge, vigilance, and will of one man;* but scarcely in an instance, save the conscriptions when the Empire was pressed for supplies of men, did that dependence on the ubiquity of the Emperor's protection and the inflexible impartiality of his administration, fail any of his subjects. Had any prefect or military man interfered with the election of deputies, nomination of juries, or common transactions of life in the way since practiced in every department, such illegal and vexatious interference would, without even the necessity of a remonstance, have been immediately punished and remedied under the Imperial government. The principles of freedom, which can alone secure good institutions from abuse, were nearly extinguished under his absolute rule, and have revived and attained some vigor since his downfall; but equality † before the law, impartiality in the administration of justice, and certainty of redress in case of any injury, either from individuals or from civil and military authorities, have not been greater or even so great under the succeeding gov-

* The following picture of Napoleon's government is taken chiefly from M. Gallois, who has frequently, and nearly in the terms of the text, given me such a representation of the justice, policy, and vigilance of his administration as I have here endeavored to preserve.

† "Le Français aime l'égalité, il ne se soucie pas beaucoup de la liberté," was the remark of Napoleon to Lord Ebrington in Elba; and if it was well founded, he certainly gave the French the government they liked.

ernments during peace, as they were under Napoleon at war with half the world. I received this remarkable testimony to the character of the Imperial government* from an unbiased and unsuspected quarter, from M. Gallois, who had refused employment under him, and was too sincere and enlightened a friend of freedom not to abhor a system which depended exclusively on the character of an individual. It was the result of observation and reflection, not of personal attachment, much less of habitual reverence for power. He admitted that the all-penetrating sagacity of Napoleon, his indefatigable diligence, his extraordinary knowledge of men and things, and his stern, inflexible impartiality, were, during his life, efficacious substitutes for much better institutions; but he justly observed that the inherent vices would, in all certainty, have been felt, as they, in fact, were, the moment that the wonderful genius which corrected them, ceased to be at the head of the state. "Je n'aime pas beaucoup les femmes, ni le jeu," said he once to my informant, "enfin rien; je suis tout-à-fait un être politique." His powers of application and memory seemed almost preternatural. There was scarcely a man in France, and none in employment, with whose private history, characters, and qualifications, he was not acquainted. He had, when Emperor, notes and tables, which he called the moral statistics of his Empire. He revised and corrected them by ministerial reports, private conversation, and correspondence. He received all letters himself, and what seems incredible,

* It was confirmed in many particulars by other sober-minded and credible men who lived under his government, and had access to him or to his ministers.

he read and recollected all that he received. He slept little, and was never idle one instant when awake. When he had an hour for diversion, he not unfrequently employed it in looking over a book of logarithms, which he acknowledged, with some surprise, was at all seasons of his life a recreation to him. So retentive was his memory of numbers, that sums over which he had once glanced his eye were in his mind ever after. He recollected the respective produce of all taxes through every year of his administration, and could, at any time, repeat any one of them, even to the centimes. Thus his detection of errors in accounts appeared marvelous, and he often indulged in the pardonable artifice of displaying these faculties in a way to create a persuasion that his vigilance was almost supernatural. In running over an account of expenditure, he perceived the rations of a battalion charged on a certain day at Besançon. "Mais le bataillon n'était pas là," said he, "il y a erreur." The minister, recollecting that the Emperor had been at the time out of France, and confiding in the regularity of his subordinate agents, persisted that the battalion must have been at Besançon. Napoleon insisted on further inquiry. It turned out to be a fraud and not a mistake. The peculating accountant was dismissed, and the scrutinizing spirit of the Emperor circulated with the anecdote through every branch of the public service, in a way to deter every clerk from committing the slightest error, from fear of immediate detection. His knowledge, in other matters, was often as accurate and nearly as surprising. Not only were the Swiss deputies in 1801 astonished at his familiar acquaintance with the history, laws, and usages of their country, which seemed the result of a life of research, but even the envoys from the insignificant republic of San Marino* were astonished at finding that he knew the families and feuds of that small community, and discoursed on the respective views, conditions and interests of parties and individuals, as if he had been educated in the petty squabbles and local politics of that diminutive society. I remember a simple native of that place told me in 1814, that the phenomenon was accounted for by the Saint of the town appearing to him over-night, in order to assist his deliberations. Some anecdotes related to me by the distinguished officer who conveyed him in the Undaunted to Elba in 1814, prove the extent, variety, and accuracy of knowledge of Napoleon. On his first arrival on the coast, in company with Sir Neil Campbell, an Austrian and a Russian commissioner, Captain Usher waited upon him, and was invited to dinner. He conversed much on naval affairs, and explained the plan he had once conceived of forming a vast fleet of 160 ships of the line. He asked Captain Usher if he did not think it would have been practicable; and Usher answered, that with the immense means he then commanded, he saw no impossibility in building and manning any number of ships, but his difficulty would have consisted in forming thorough seamen, as distinguished from what we call smooth-water sailors. Napoleon replied that he had provided for that also; he had organized exercises for them afloat, not only in harbor, but in smaller vessels near the coast, by which they might have been trained to go through, even in rough

* They waited upon him at Bologna.

weather, the most arduous manœuvres of seamanship which he enumerated; and he mentioned among them the keeping a ship clear of her anchors in a heavy sea. The Austrian, who suspected Napoleon of talking in general upon subjects he imperfectly understood, acknowledging his own ignorance, asked him the meaning of the term, the nature of the difficulty, and the method of surmounting it. On this the Emperor took up two forks, and explained the problem in seamanship, which is not an easy one, in so short, scientific, and practical a way, that Captain Usher assured me he knew none but professional men, and very few of them, who could off-hand have given a so perspicuous, seamanlike, and satisfactory solution of the question. Any board of officers would have inferred, from such an exposition, that the person making it had received a naval education, and was a practical seaman. Yet how different were the objects on which the mind of Napoleon must have been long, as well as recently, employed!

On the same voyage, when the propriety of putting into a harbor* of Corsica was under discussion, and the want of a pilot urged as an objection, Napoleon described the depth of water, shoals, currents, bearings, and anchorage, with a minuteness which seemed as if he had himself acted in that capacity; and which, on reference to the charts, was found scrupulously accurate. When his cavalry and baggage arrived at Porto Farajo, the commander of the transports said that he had been on the point of putting into a creek near Genoa (which he named, but I have

* I think Bastia.

forgotten); upon hearing which Napoleon exclaimed, "It is well you did not; it is the worst place in the Mediterranean; you would not have got to sea again for a month or six weeks." He then proceeded to allege reasons for the difficulty, which were quite sufficient, if the peculiarities of the little bay were really such as he described; but Captain Usher, having never heard of them during his service in the Mediterranean, suspected that the Emperor was mistaken, or had confounded some report he had heard from mariners in his youth. When, however, he mentioned the circumstance, many years afterward, to Captain Dundas, who had recently cruised in the Gulf of Genoa, that officer confirmed the report of Napoleon in all its particulars, and expressed astonishment at its correctness. "For" (said he) "I thought it a discovery of my own, having ascertained all you have just told me about that creek, by observation and experience."* Great as was his appetite for knowledge, his memory in retaining, and his quickness in applying it, his labor both in acquiring and using it was equal to them. In application to business he could wear out the men most inured to study. In the deliberations on the Code Civil, many of which lasted ten, twelve or fifteen hours without intermission, he was always the last whose attention flagged; and he was so little disposed to spare himself trouble, that even in the Moscow campaign he sent regularly to every branch of administration in Paris directions in detail, which in every government but his would, both from usage and convenience, have been left to the discretion of the super-

* Related to me by Captain Usher at Paris, 1826.

intending minister, or to the common routine of business. This and other instances of his diligence are more wonderful than praiseworthy. He had established an office with twelve clerks and Mounier at their head, whose sole duty it was to extract, translate, abridge, and arrange under heads the contents of our English newspapers. He charged Mounier to omit no abuse of him, however coarse or virulent; no charge, however injurious or malignant. As, however, he did not specify the Empress, Mounier, who reluctantly complied with his orders, ventured to suppress, or at least to soften, any phrases about her; but Napoleon questioned others on the contents of the English papers; detected Mounier and his committee in their mutilations of the articles, and forbade them to withold any intelligence or any censure they met with in the publications which they were appointed to examine. Yet with all this industry, and with the multiplicity of topics which engaged his attention, he found time for private and various reading. His librarian was employed for some time every morning in replacing maps and books which his unwearied and insatiable curiosity had consulted before breakfast. He read all letters whatever addressed to himself, whether in his private or public capacity; and it must, I believe, be acknowledged that he often took the same liberty with those directed to other people. He had indulged in that unjustifiable practice* before his elevation, and such was his impatience to open both parcels and letters that, however employed, he could seldom defer the gratification of his curiosity an instant after

* Denon, Mechin, and others.

either came under his notice or his reach. Josephine, and others, well acquainted with his habits, very pardonably took some advantage of this propensity. Matters which she feared to mention to him were written and directed to her, and the letters unopened left in his way. He often complied with wishes which he thought he had detected by an artifice, more readily than had they been presented in the form of claim, petition, or request. He liked to know every thing; but he liked all he did to have the appearance of springing entirely from himself, feeling, like many others in power, an unwillingness to encourage even those they love in an opinion that they have an influence over them, or that there is any certain channel to their favor. His childish eagerness about cases, led in one instance to a gracious act of playful munificence. He received notice of the arrival of a present from Constantinople, in society with the Empress and other ladies. He ordered the parcel* to be brought up, and instantly tore it open with his own hand. It contained a large aigrette of diamonds, which he broke into various pieces, and he then threw the largest into her Imperial Majesty's lap, and some into that of every lady in the circle.

With the temper and habits I have described, he was not likely to be scrupulous in furnishing his police with much vexatious authority. It was accordingly most active and most odious; but such has always been and is still the practice in France. Napoleon's agents were for the most part restored emigrants, ex-nobles, and pretended Royalists. Many, after the restoration, were indiscreet

* Mechin.

enough to acknowledge or at least to prove by their complaints of the niggardly boons which they received from Louis XVIII., that the profit derived from betraying the cause of legitimacy under the Usurper had exceeded what they earned by their support of it under a Bourbon prince. Napoleon restored, with the exception of forests, all lands that were not sold before his accession to power. He gave the proprietors of such restored land their full share of office, favor, and power under his government, and he left the few who were unwilling to serve him unmolested in the enjoyment of their estates. Extensive as the confiscations during the Revolution were, the barbarous law of corruption of blood was unknown in France, and the rights of those relations who had neither emigrated nor been condemned by any tribunal remained inviolate. This circumstance, together with the restitutions of lands under the Directory and Napoleon, and of the forests under the Bourbons, has rendered the change in real property* much less extensive in France than is generally supposed. Much, indeed, has been divided by the operation of the law of inheritance; but in those cases it still remains in branches of the family of the original possessor. The richest proprietors of France are still to be found among the nobles who bore arms against their country, or their descendants and relations; and the whole mass of confiscated land not now in possession of the families to whom it belonged in 1793, or of those to whom those families

* My observation is of course confined to real property of a private nature. All church and many corporation lands were sold or otherwise alienated, and none, I presume, have been directly or indirectly restored.

have sold it, would not amount to the value of property lost by confiscation in Ireland by the single family of Fitzgerald. Napoleon, especially during the first years of his Imperial government, hazarded more from his disposition to reconcile the old nobility to his dynasty, than from any other partiality. A large portion of what he gave privately fell to their share, sometimes as objects of munificence and charity, sometimes as spies and secret agents both abroad and at home. Meanwhile, the Jacobins, excluded by him from all ostensible office, remained (with the exception of Barère, and one or two other names polluted by corruption as well as stained with blood) in the poverty which, it must be acknowledged, their possession of power never had altered. Many leading men during the reign of Terror, and several of the Directors and their ministers, lived, long after their retreat, in obscurity and penury, without having contracted the habits of expense or acquired the means of indulging it, from the possession of a large share of the government of a rich and extensive empire.* Truth should be told even of demons. The Jacobins, sanguinary as they were, are calumniated when a love of rapine is added to the catalogue of their iniquities. Even the cowardly and cruel Robespierre was pure about money; and the general character of that disorganizing party was a disdain of luxury and wealth. The fortunes of Napoleon's ministers and marshals have been in like manner grossly exaggerated by his detractors. Some turned out small after their death, and the largest were derived almost exclusively from foreign plunder or

* The concluding words of Mr. Pitt's epitaph are applicable to nearly all of them: "*They died poor.*"

foreign servility. The Princes of the Continent, when stooping to solicit a share of that spoil of dominion which Napoleon's victories had procured him, resorted to those means which they knew to be most prevalent and most efficacious in their own legitimate and unprincipled courts. They furthered or hoped to further their selfish designs by presents, bribes, and flattery to the ministers and favorites of that man whom they have since spoken of as an upstart and usurper, unfit to be admitted into their princely society! He possibly connived at the practice. He most justly and cordially despised the pusillanimous creatures who resorted to it. He sometimes treated them* with rudeness and insolence. He on one occasion dined with his hat on, when three kings and several sovereign princes sat uncovered at table. Returning from the chase with the Kings of Saxony, Wurtemberg, and Bavaria in the carriage, he stopped at the Malmaison to pay a private visit to his divorced wife, Josephine, and kept the monarchs waiting at least an hour at the door. The King of Bavaria who recounted the story to my informant was more diverted than affronted at the incident, and said, "Puisqu'on nous traite comme des lacquais, il faut nous divertir comme tels," and asking for bread, cheese, fruit and wine, regaled himself with that homely cheer in the

* "Have we not seen his morning chamber fill'd
With sceptred slaves who waited to salute him?
Menial Kings
Ran coursing up and down his palace yard,
Stood silent in his presence, watched his eyes,
And at his least command all started out
Like racers to the goal." *All for Love.*

carriage or in the hall, with admirable good-humor and excellent appetite. Such or similar improprieties were not unusual at his Imperial court. The ill-breeding generated in camps and in clubs, and the dry, undignified formality which often disfigures the manners of official men, were discernible in his drawing-room and ante-chamber; but there was no appearance and very little reality in the dissoluteness of manners attributed by our ignorant libelists to his family and favorites. I have heard of his amours. They were neither frequent nor scandalous. A Polish lady and Mademoiselle George, the actress, have been mentioned. He had a son by the former, and some pretend that he left two natural children by some other woman. But on the whole, his court, if not the most refined or agreeable, was the least immoral and dissipated known in France for three centuries. He encouraged his marshals, generals, and ministers to marry, and was desirous they should form alliances with the families of the ancient nobility. On the other hand, he set his face against ill-assorted marriages in age, fortune, or station. There was a story that he had collected the names of all the heiresses in his dominions, with the intention of bestowing them, even against their will, on his favorite officers or dependents.

But many projects that passed through his inventive mind were more abruptly started in conversation by him, and afterward repeated as deliberate designs by his courtiers and injudicious admirers. If liable to strong objections in principle, they were, after his downfall, confidently stated by his calumniators to have been measures in contemplation or in the course of completion by the Imperial

Government. Thus, an idea of confining the study of all schools, universities, and public institutions to a regulated number of books printed and published by authority, and an intention to burn all others, and reduce the Bibliothèque Impériale and every public library to the legal number, was gravely imputed to him by writers, orators,* and flatterers, who found their interest in propagating calumnies against fallen greatness. His conversation, in truth, was full of projects, sometimes merely fanciful for the exercise of his unwearied understanding, sometimes for the purpose of sounding the opinions of others on schemes for which he had an inclination, and sometimes for that of really organizing and promoting the gigantic designs he had conceived. "Il produisait beaucoup," said M. de Talleyrand to me. "C'est incalculable ce qu'il produisait, plus qu'aucun homme, oui, plus qu'aucun quatre hommes que j'aie jamais connus. Son génie était inconcevable. Rien n'égalait son énergie, son imagination, son esprit, sa capacité de travail, sa facilité de produire. Il avait de la sagacité aussi. Du coté du jugement il n'était pas si fort; mais encore *quand il vouloit se donner le temps* il savoit profiter du jugement des autres. Ce n'était que rarement que son mauvais jugement l'emportait, et c'était toujours lorsqu'il ne s'étoit pas donné le temps de consulter celui d'autres personnes."

Among his projects were many connected with the arts and with literature. They were all, perhaps, subservient to political purposes, generally gigantic, abruptly prepared,

* Even Lord Liverpool condescended to allude to this foolish imputation, and gravely stated in the House that the interests of literature required the downfall of Napoleon

and in all likelihood as suddenly conceived. Many were topics of conversation and subjects for speculation, not serious, practical, or digested designs. Though not insensible to the arts or to literature, he was suspected latterly of considering them rather as political engines or embellishments than as sources of enjoyment. M. de Talleyrand, and several artists, concurred in saying that "il avait le sentiment du Grand, mais non pas celui du Beau." He had written "bon sujet d'un tableau," opposite to some passage in Letourneur's translation of Ossian, and he had certainly a passion for that poem. His censure on David, for choosing the battle at the Straits of Thermopylæ as a subject for a picture, was that of a general rather than connoisseur: it smelt, if I may say so, of his shop; though perhaps the real motive for it was dislike to the republican artist, and distaste to an act of national resistance against a great military invader. "A bad subject," said he; "after all, Leonidas was turned." He had the littleness to expect to be prominent in every picture of national victories of his time, and was displeased at a painting of an action in Egypt for Madame Murat, in which her wounded husband was the principal figure. Power made him impatient of contradiction,* even in trifles; and latterly he did not like his taste in music, for which he had no turn, to be disputed. His proficiency in literature has been variously stated.

* He was not so, however, either in deliberation or discussion, at least when the latter was invited by himself. He allowed his ministers to comment upon, and even to object to measures in contemplation (provided they acquiesced in them when adopted) in free and even strong terms, and he liked those he questioned on facts or opinions to answer without compliment or reserve.

He had read much, but had written little. In the mechanical part he was certainly no adept; his handwriting was nearly illegible. Some would fain persuade me that that fault was intentional, and merely an artifice to conceal his bad spelling; that he could form his letters well if he chose, but was unwilling to let his readers know too exactly the use he made of them. His orthography was certainly not correct; that of few Frenchmen, not professed authors, was so, thirty years ago: but his brothers Lucien and Louis, both literary men, and both correct in their orthography, write a similar hand, and nearly as bad a one as he did, probably for the same reason; viz., that they can not write a better without great pains and loss of time.

Napoleon, when Consul and Emperor, seldom wrote, but he dictated much. It was difficult to follow him, and he often objected to any revision of what he had dictated. When a word had escaped his amanuensis, and he was asked what it was, he would answer somewhat pettishly,* "Je ne répéterai pas le mot. Réfléchissez, rappelez vous du mot que j'ai dicté, et écrivez-le, car pour moi je ne le répéterai pas." Talleyrand, interested possibly in discrediting any posthumous writings, was very earnest, soon after the news of his death arrived, in inculcating on me and others the persuasion that Napoleon never did and never could dictate. "Il disait, il ne dictait pas; on ne pouvait écrire sous sa dictée. Il ne sçavait ni dicter ni écrire." But, excepting Talleyrand and Charles IV. of Spain, I never heard any one express a doubt of his powers of composition, or his habits of dictating. It was,

* General Bertrand and Cambacérès.

indeed, difficult to follow, and yet more difficult to satisfy him in the discharge of that office; but M. Bignon and others* inured themselves to his manner. In matters of importance he would look over and correct what had been written from his dictation, and would afterward repeat word for word the sentences he had composed and revised. His style was clear. "Soyez clair, tout le reste viendra," was a maxim of his. In matters of business he very justly ridiculed and defied that absurd canon of French criticism which forbids the recurrence of a word twice in the same sentence or even page. He had several volumes of his correspondence copied out and bound in folio. There is some mystery attending the fate of those books. From them, however, the "lettres inédites" were published. M. de Talleyrand pretends that his copies sometimes varied, and that purposely, from the originals, for according to him Napoleon would not scruple, even in transcribing treaties, to substitute one word for another. The notes on the life of the Duke of Marlborough, which was printed at his expense, and by his desire, were, it is said, composed by him, and paragraphs of his writing were occasionally inserted in the newspaper. He wrote and printed when a young man, at Avignon, in 1793 or 1794, a small political pamphlet, called "Déjeuner de trois Militaires," and I have already mentioned that he sent a manuscript history of Corsica, written before that period, to Abbé Raynal. But whatever were his own writings, his criticism on the works of others was generally just, and always striking and acute. Le Mercier read him a play on the subject of

* My authorities are numerous: Cambacérès, Barbé-Marbois, Daru, Las Casas, Bertrand, and many more.

Peter the Cruel. At the moment of his fall, that discomfited tyrant was made to say something like this:

"De tout mon vaste empire, il me reste un rocher."

Napoleon observed, "it will *never* do. You mean to rouse us to indignation against the man, and you put in his mouth a pathetic remark on the contrast between his former elevation and present ruin, that can not fail to excite the compassion of every well-regulated mind." The remark was subtle, and considering subsequent events curious and singular. It is possible, however, that this latter circumstance produced it, for the relator, though a worthy man, was a dramatic author. In reading, Napoleon leant to skepticism and paradox; as, for instance, he ridiculed as improbable the story of Cæsar's escape in the boat, and his speech to the boatman, and was much inclined to disparage the talents and more particularly the military skill of that extraordinary man.

I have seen the official correspondence with Caulincourt when he was employed at Châtillon in 1814. It gave me the highest opinion of the abilities, integrity, and pacific principles of that negotiator. It did not, I confess, raise my opinion of the Emperor Napoleon. It was full of subterfuge and artifice on the part of the government. There seemed an intention not only of violating faith with the confederates, but in case of need, of disavowing and sacrificing the honor of the negotiator, who was serving his country with zeal, talent, and fidelity. Caulincourt reasonably and honestly endeavored to work on the predilections of Austria to procure good terms of peace for Napoleon, but that prince and his immediate advisers were more disposed to avail themselves of any favorable disposition in Austria to sow dissensions.* They were obviously anxious to obtain credit with France for wishing and promoting peace, but not much disposed either to obtain, or if obtained, to preserve it. In the mean while, the partisans of peace at Paris were not only prepared, but much disposed to sacrifice Napoleon himself to that object, which his negotiator, Caulincourt, was equally determined not to do. M. de Talleyrand and the Duke Dalberg fixed on M. de Vitrolles† (a bad man, long in emigration, and the author of the note secrète in 1818) to convey to the Austrians their desire to learn what conditions would be imposed on France, if France were to agree to dethrone and abandon Napoleon. Neither M. de Talleyrand nor his coadjutors were aware that the man they employed in this delicate mission was already the agent of Monsieur and the Bourbons. They had from caution refrained from writing,‡

* Of these Maret, Duke of Bassano, a well meaning and intelligent, but time-serving and obsequious man, and Savary, one of the vilest instruments of Napoleon, were, I believe, the chiefs.

† I have related the same story nearly in the same words in Chap. vii. Part ii. B. of MS. Memoirs. That relation was taken from notes written in 1821, and the text here is transcribed, with such emendations or additions as subsequent information has supplied in Paris, in 1826, from the original notes.

‡ Some say he had a ring which Talleyrand had received from Metternich. Pozzo di Borgo told me he had also two or three insignificant words in the Duke *Dalberg's handwriting*, with which Metternich or Nesselrode was acquainted, which words were concealed in a button; and Lord Goderich told me (in January, 1833), that Vitrolles brought with him a note of invitation or civility in Lord Castlereagh's handwriting to the Princesse de Vaudemont, as part of

and Talleyrand only gave him some trifles which Prince Metternich would recognize, and which would serve for a proof of his being the bearer of a message. When he arrived at Châtillon, the Allies were exasperated at the bad faith of Napoleon, and determined to exact some change as the price of peace from France, but not determined what that revolution or counter-revolution should be. Austria, who had been the most backward in sacrificing Napoleon, was still averse to restoring a family which would exclude Maria Louisa and her son from all hopes of the succession. In these dispositions she was strengthened by observing the silence of all parts of France, with the solitary exception of Bordeaux, and the oblivion and contempt into which the cause and name of the Bourbons had obviously fallen. But Vitrolles had the address to remove such objections. He converted his mission of inquiry into one of communication, and having produced his credentials of handwriting or trinkets, assured the Allies that M. de Talleyrand and others had formed their plot, were determined to restore the Bourbons, and anxiously expecting the armies at Paris, and a declaration in favor of the exiled family. When the armies arrived, the Allies*

the proof of his being confidentially intrusted by persons connected with Talleyrand and his party in Paris. Any or all of these specific signs may have been adopted, but it is unquestionable that they or some such were resorted to.

* Pozzo di Borgo and others have confirmed this and some other parts of the narrative. The whole comes to me *indirectly* from the Duke Dalberg. I believe I have related it elsewhere in these papers, but *stet.*

Alexander had some inclination to place Bernadotte on the throne of France: several persons better acquainted with the dispositions of Frenchmen leaned to the Duke of Orleans; but Austria considered were much surprised to find no such conspiracy organized, and Talleyrand no less so that his name had been instrumental in restoring the Bourbons. He was, however, too quick-sighted not to make a virtue of necessity. The restoration was inevitable, and he was too adroit not to father the spurious child which had been unexpectedly sworn to him by the prostitute who had conceived it.

At Elba, Napoleon seemed absorbed in domestic details, the arrangement of the petty concerns of the place, and the reception of his English visitors. To several of the latter he spoke with earnestness and freedom of passing and past events. The short printed narrative of Lord Ebrington is one of the happiest and most authentic representations of the spirit, character, and interest of his conversation. Sir Neil Campbell was strangely deceived in his estimate of his general character, as in his view of his immediate designs. I heard him myself declare that his talents did not seem to him superior to those which would be required in a sous-prefet! Some imagine that he lulled that officer into security by purposely concealing* his intellectual qualifications as well as his actual designs. It is notorious that Sir Neil was overwhelmed with surprise at his departure from Porto Ferraio. The ridicule to which his want

Napoleon or Louis XVIII. as the sole alternative, and our Regent, though not his ministers, were invariably for Louis. See Appendix No. VII., respecting the elevation of Louis-Philippe to the throne in 1830.

* I suspect Sir Neil was misled by his own simplicity, by the preconceived opinions which newspapers and libels had created in his mind, and by that propensity so common in official men to believe and to circulate whatever tends to gratify the prejudice or the malignity of their employers.

of vigilance exposed him had a pernicious effect afterward on the nerves of Sir Hudson Lowe, and contributed to induce that more ostensible jailer to adopt a system more irksome to his great prisoner, and more discreditable to England than even the narrow policy of our councils had intended.

There can be little doubt that a conspiracy was forming in the French army at the beginning of the year 1815 for expelling the House of Bourbon. The leaders, however, neither invited nor intended to invite Napoleon to put himself at the head of their party. He probably ascertained the existence of the plot, and was aware that there was no wish to concert it with him. But encouraged by the respect his name still inspired in the soldiery, alarmed at his own precarious situation, and of reports of the designs at the Congress of Vienna, and urged by the natural impatience and ambition of his character, he certainly landed before any such conspiracy was ripe, and seized prematurely, and for his own use, the greater part of the materials of which any successful conspiracy could be formed. He soon perceived that the strength of his cause lay both in a party and in principles more republican than he had ever favored or encouraged. How far he wavered between his former system of government and the establishment of one more popular in its spirit as well as form, and how far such fluctuation of counsel, so unlike all his former conduct, was produced by change of situation and character, and ultimately overwhelmed him in ruin, are interesting inquiries for the historian. They would lead me too far. He felt his embarrassment during the hundred days. Count Molé, who is no tribune of the people, told me that

Napoleon expressed great apprehensions that the republican party would prevail; that he spoke of scenes he had witnessed in the revolution with disgust and emotion; that he drew with great sagacity, but with some bitterness, the characters of the marshals, ministers, and demagogues who surrounded him; lamented the impossibility of raising France to resistance against the confederates without resorting to means which he had always reprobated;* and acknowledged that had he foreseen how much compliance with the democratic party was necessary to his support, he would never have left the Island of Elba. He added that his chief hopes of extricating France from her internal and external dangers depended on the cordial co-operation of such sober-minded men as my informant. From such a moral in the conclusion, some of my shrewder readers may infer, and possibly be right in inferring, that the whole conversation proved Napoleon's knowledge of individual character much more than his fears of democracy generally, or at that epoch in particular. Whatever was his object, he unquestionably held this language; for the person to whom he addressed it is too distinct to forget, and too correctly honorable to be capable of misrepresentation.

His life, occupations, health, and conversation in his exile at St. Helena have been so minutely and so frequently described in print, that, in preserving notes of what has been told me by his inmates at Longwood, I may be repeating what is well known and undisputed. He occasionally played at chess and at billiards, at the first with tolerable skill, but intolerable rapidity; at the latter, neither with mace nor cue, but with his hand. Before he had

* Qu'il avait toujours désapprouvés.

regulated the distribution of his time, he was very anxious not to be left between dinner and the hour of retiring to rest. To prevent the ladies from retiring, he would sit long at table, exert himself to keep up conversation, and sometimes send for books to read aloud to the company. He read well, but he read the same poems and same plays too frequently. Among the latter, Zaire was his favorite lecture. He slept himself when read to, but he was very observant and jealous if others slept while he read. He watched his audience vigilantly, and "Madame Montholon, vous dormez," was a frequent ejaculation in the course of reading. He was animated with all that he read, especially poetry; enthusiastic at beautiful passages, impatient and observant of faults, and full of ingenious and lively remarks on style, composition, and story. He read through the Odyssey, I presume in Dacier's translation, and the Bible. He could hardly get through the first for the comments it excited, and, as he had not been very conversant with the Old Testament, he was alternately surprised and delighted, provoked and diverted, at the sublimity and beauty of some passages, and what appeared to him the extravagance and absurdity of others. He expressed all these emotions with great freedom and eagerness; and the manner as well as matter of his remarks awakened and fixed the attention of his audience. In the long evenings passed thus in conversation, reading, criticism, and narrative, he not only took a prominent part, but was so luminous and earnest, and yet so philosophical, calm, and above resentment in describing the events of his life, and drawing the portraits of those with whom he had passed it, that Madame Montholon, with great felicity, compared the sensations of the company to those of a future state, in which they were taking a dispassionate view of the transactions of the world in which they had been engaged. Napoleon was curious about all new books which arrived at St. Helena. Without understanding English well, or speaking it at all, he could make out histories and read newspapers and reviews in our language. He grew so conversant in the latter, that on the arrival of the Edinburgh and Quarterly, he made very plausible conjectures about the authors of the articles in each publication. That on Warden's book * puzzled and perplexed him exceedingly, but did not displease him. The anecdotes of his early life, derived through me from Cardinal Fesch and Louis Bonaparte, quite astonished him. "Where on earth have they been to hunt out that? but I recollect it. Where on earth could those English fellows get at it?" His indefatigable mind, which found matter for inquiry and speculation in every thing, was not exempt from the failing to which such active spirits are liable, of discovering more than exists, of working upon plain materials not susceptible of such refinement, in short, to use the homely proverb, of *seeing too far into a mill-stone.* Lady Holland had prevailed on the Duke of Bedford to send Napoleon a book. He left the choice of it to her, and she delayed it till the day before the ship was to sail. She consequently requested a friend to purchase the first well-bound book that came to hand in the bookseller's shop, and as it was a Scotch hand that it came to, Robertson's History of Scotland was naturally enough the book selected. "Why does the Duke of Bedford send me the History of Scotland?

* It was written by Mr. Allen.

He must know that I have read it. Oh, εὕρηκα, he means to hint to me never to acknowledge, like Mary, Queen of Scots, the jurisdiction of England." Another book, Coxe's life of the Duke of Marlborough, sent to him by Lord Robert Spenser, a descendant of that great man, delighted him much. He wished in his last moments to convey it as no unappropriate memorial to an English regiment in the island, whose officers possessed a library, and had been remarkably civil to him. He requested Dr. Arnott, their surgeon, who had attended him, to present it; but Dr. Arnott was ordered by his superiors to return the book, first, because it had not been transmitted through the Government House; secondly, because it was in the name of the Emperor Napoleon, not of General Bonaparte. Pitiful, narrow-minded malignity, disgraceful alike to the government and its agents!

General Bertrand had applied to our Government for Folard's Polybius, but it was not furnished. Napoleon was somewhat impatient for its arrival, but it was only during the latter months of his life that he obtained it, I believe, from Lady Holland. He read it incessantly, and spoke of the ancient author with great admiration. His habits and regimen during his whole life, and more particularly in his exile at St. Helena, were singular; he ate little and rapidly, dined early, and not unfrequently neglected breakfast altogether; he drank, when well, light French wines, and especially Lunel, but never to excess. In his illness, and for some time before, he lost his appetite entirely, though Lady Holland had the satisfaction of learning that the confectionery she had sent him was much approved. Indeed, some preserves which he called "pruneaux de Madame Holland," were nearly the last article of food he ever asked for. At St. Helena, he rose at four, and throughout his life was accustomed to get up for an hour, if not two, in the course of the night; and, as he had always two beds in the room, was very frequently found to have changed them before morning. The habit of interrupting his rest with an interval of watchfulness was probably contracted during his campaigns, and it was of great use to him when on service. He explained and directed, with a clear head, after his first sleep, all the general arrangements of the ensuing day; and then, after a second and refreshing repose, superintended the execution of them, without the possibility of the more ordinary business interrupting the last orders necessary to be given.

Many curious details of the decline of his health, the nature of his disease, and his own sagacious and characteristic remarks on the cause and treatment of it, may be collected from the publications of his various medical attendants, among whom it became, unfortunately, a subject of much painful controversy. His father had died of a scirrhus in the pylorus; his sister, the Princess Borghese, has more recently fallen a victim to a similar disease. It is not likely that the climate could cause the disorder; but the dampness of that part of the island which he inhabited, the vexation occasioned by exile and confinement, and the absence of his family, and of such assistance as he could have commanded in Europe,* may have accelerated his death, and unquestionably aggravated his sufferings. He was at all times disposed to converse

* If it be granted that his disease was incurable, it can not be denied that any officer on service, in the state of health under which he labored for two years, would have had leave to return to Europe for medical advice.

on metaphysical subjects, and curious in questioning well-informed priests on the foundation and nature of their faith. He was consequently disappointed on finding that the two ecclesiastics sent out to St. Helena, though selected by Cardinal Fesch, were men of limited understandings, and no reading at all. The old man, Buonavita, though his adventures in Spain, Mexico, and New York, might afford some amusement, was grossly ignorant. He told Napoleon that he resembled the most able and fortunate of all *Roman* generals, namely *Alexander the Great.* Whether it be true or not that the Emperor condemned him for that historical blunder to read ten pages of Rollin every morning, and to repeat the substance of his lesson to him,* he was certainly indignant that so uninteresting a companion had been appointed to attend him.

Whatever were the religious sentiments of this extraordinary man, such companions were likely neither to fix nor to shake, to sway nor to alter them. I have been at some pains to ascertain the little that can be known of his thoughts on such subjects; and though it is not very satisfactory, it appears to me worth recording.

In the early periods of the revolution, he, in common with many of his conntrymen, conformed to the fashion of treating all such matters, both in conversation and action, with levity and even derision. In his subsequent career, like most men exposed to wonderful vicissitudes, he professed, half in jest and half in earnest, a sort of confidence in fatalism and predestination. But on some solemn pub-

* I believe this story to be a perversion of another fact. Napoleon liked his younger chaplain, and finding that his education had been neglected, recommended books to him, and in some sort superintended his course of study.

lic occasions, and yet more in private and sober discussion, he not only gravely disclaimed and reproved infidelity, but both by actions and words implied his conviction that a conversion to religious enthusiasm might befall himself or any other man. He had more than tolerance—he had indulgence and respect—for extravagant ascetic notions of religious duty. He grounded that feeling not on their soundness or their truth, but on the uncertainty of what our minds may be reserved for, on the possibility of our being prevailed upon to admit and even to devote ourselves to tenets which at first excite our derision. It has been observed that there was a tincture* of Italian superstition in his character, a sort of conviction from reason that the doctrines of revelation were not true, and yet a persuasion, or at least an apprehension, that he might live to think them so. He was satisfied that the seeds of belief were deeply sown in the human heart. It was on that principle that he permitted and justified, though he did not dare to authorize the revival of La Trappe† and other austere orders. He contended that they might operate as a safety-valve for the fanatical and visionary ferment which would otherwise burst forth and disturb society. In his remarks on the death of Duroc‡ and in the reasons he alleged against suicide, both in calm and speculative discussion and in moments of strong emotion (such as occurred at Fontainebleau§ in 1814), he implied a belief both in fatality and providence.

* Pasquier, Stan. Girardin, and others. † Molé.

‡ See Lord Ebrington's narrative.

§ General Sebastiani and Comte Flahault: *aussi ne suis-je pas tout-à-fait étranger à des idées religieuses,* added he, after assigning worldly reasons for not killing himself.

In the programme of his coronation, a part of the ceremony was to consist in his taking the communion. But when the plan was submitted to him, he, to the surprise of those who had drawn it, was absolutely indignant* at the suggestion. "No man," he said, "had the means of knowing, or had the right to say, when or where he would take the Sacrament, or whether he would or not." On this occasion, he added that he would not,† nor did he!

There is some mystery about his conduct in similar respects at St. Helena, and during the last days of his life. He certainly had mass celebrated in his chapel while he was well, and in his bedroom when ill. But though I have reason to believe that the last Sacraments were actually administered to him privately, a few days before his death, and probably after confession, yet Count Montholon, from whom I derive indirectly my information, also stated that he received Napoleon's earnest and distinct directions to conceal all the preliminary preparations for that melancholy ceremony from all his other companions, and even to enjoin the priest, if questioned, to say he acted by Count Montholon's orders, but had no knowledge of the Emperor's wishes.

It seems as if he had some desire for such assurance as the Church could give, but yet was ashamed to own it. He knew that some at St. Helena, and more in France, would deem his recourse to such consolation infirmity; perhaps he deemed it so himself. Religion may sing her triumph, Philosophy exclaim, "pauvre humanité," more

* Gallois, confirmed by many others.

† Some attributed this repugnance to conform, to his fear of the army, others to a secret and conscientious aversion to what he deemed in his heart a profanation.

impartial skepticism despair of discovering the motive, but truth and history must, I believe, acknowledge the fact. M. de Talleyrand, who, on hearing of his death, spoke of his mental endowments, as has been related above,* added the following remarks:

"His career is the most extraordinary that has occurred for one thousand years. He committed three capital faults, and to them his fall, scarce less extraordinary than his elevation, is to be ascribed—Spain, Russia, and the Pope. I say the Pope; for his coronation, the acknowledgment by the spiritual head of Christendom that he, a little lieutenant of Corsica, was the chief sovereign of Europe, *from* whatever motive it proceeded, was the most striking consummation of glory that could happen to an individual. After adopting that mode of displaying his greatness and crowning his achievements, he should never, for objects comparatively insignificant, have stooped to vex and persecute the same Pontiff. He thereby outraged the feelings of the very persons whose enmity had been softened, and whose imagination had been dazzled by that brilliant event. Such were his capital errors. Those three apart, he committed few others in policy, wonderfully few, considering the multiplicity of interests he had to manage, and the extent, importance, and rapidity of the events in which he was engaged. He was certainly a great, an extraordinary man, nearly as extraordinary in his qualities as in his career; at least, so upon reflection I, who have seen him near and much, am disposed to con-

* On one occasion, Talleyrand said of him to me emphatically "il étoit mal élevé;" and he more than once repeated and maintained, what I fear is but too well founded, that he had very little regard for truth.

sider him. He was clearly the most extraordinary man I ever saw, and I believe the most extraordinary man that has lived in our age, or for many ages."

Another and perhaps a more fatal fault than any of the three so justly imputed to him by Talleyrand was acknowledged* by Napoleon himself in his conversations at Elba. This was the neglecting to make peace after the victories of Lutzen and Bautzen, in 1813. Those successes would have enabled him to sue for peace, much more to accept or to grant it with honor and a good grace. He might even then have obtained and almost commanded terms which would have left him the greatest potentate in Europe, and one of the most successful conquerors modern history can record. But he thought himself stronger than he was; and found himself, as he admitted, wrong in his calculations. Such mistakes and such admissions of them perhaps make him yet more extraordinary, as unquestionably the opportunity which his reverses and his exile in Elba and in St. Helena gave him of reviewing and discussing his whole conduct, of which he so amply availed himself, must and will render his life more interesting and more instructive to posterity than that of any great military prince since Julius Cæsar.

* To Mr. Fazakerley, a man of strict veracity and accurate memory who saw him in Elba, in 1814, and who has often related this part of his conversation to me. Fazakerley, on being pressed by him to make free criticisms on his conduct, expressed his surprise that he had not made peace at that epoch. "Mais je me croyais assez fort (said he) pour ne pas la faire, *et je me suis trompé*, sans cela c'était assurément le moment de faire la paix."

APPENDIX.

No. I.

(See page 23.)

Lady Holland and Mr. Allen saw in 1825 the original of this will, in the King's own hand, at the Hotel Soubise, where it was kept together with other archivès, and the celebrated iron closet found in the Tuileries in August, 1792.

The authenticity of the will has sometimes been disputed, but there seems no doubt that it is genuine. Indeed it was published immediately on that Prince's execution by his *enemies and accusers*, not by his *friends and partisans.* I remember Talleyrand explained this fact to me in much detail, and made a very just remark thereupon, that it was a strong proof of the blindness and zeal of the Jacobin party, or of the state of exaltation and republican fanaticism of the public mind at the time, when such a document, entirely in the power of the municipality, was eagerly published instead of being suppressed, from a notion that the circulation of it would injure the cause of Royalty, and expose the memory and principles of the King to the derision of his readers. Strange indeed must have been the infatuation of those who deemed such sentiments discreditable to the writer!

The expression attributed to Abbé Edgeworth of "Fils de St. Louis, montez au ciel," when the unfortunate Prince hesitated in mounting the scaffold, was an entire fiction. Abbé Edgeworth openly and honestly acknowledged he never remembered using it, and it was invented at a supper that very evening.

No. II.

(See page 70.)

19th September, 1838.

I saw the Prince of the Peace much altered in appearance, but still the same character of countenance. Good-humored, self-satisfied, somewhat jovial and hearty, in his bad French and chuckling voice, and an arch expression in his eyes, complained much of the ingratitude of the world, and included, somewhat unreasonably, in his censure that of the French government from which he receives his only subsistence, scanty indeed, but still a subsistence, 5000 francs = £200 per annum; but he contrasted it with the various sums he had in Spain allowed to the emigrant and exiled princes and noblemen of France. He complained bitterly of the Tudo, to whom he said he had been attached from his youth, to whom he had sacrificed every thing, and for whom he had incurred the (I think he said ludicrous or absurd) imputation of bigamy, and whom all the world knew he had actually married after the death of his first wife, for the purpose of legitimating her son. He had settled on her all he had in the world out of Spain, and she had left him and taken the whole, so that he was reduced to absolute penury, and lived entirely on the small pension *Luis Felipe* allowed him; for as to his estates and encomiendas, they had been distributed in a strange way. His Soto di Roma, at least all that was given to him of it by Charles IV., had been bestowed, as a national mark of gratitude and reward on the Duke of Wellington, who, he said, had earned it or any thing else; but yet, as he knew of no sentence or judgment of law depriving *him* of it, and of no proofs that disqualified him from holding it, he could not but consider it as a *despojo:* with regard to the *bienes libres* (*les biens libres*) appertaining to it (by which I understood some lands and tenements contiguous or in the neighborhood which he had purchased with his own money) they had been, by some arbitrary, but he believed formal act of one of the governments, settled on his daughter by the Bourbon wife. As to the Albufera and his encomiendas, those had been conferred on the Infante Don Francisco; so that whenever he claimed his lands he found some one in the enjoyment of them whom he had little chance of dispossessing. He rather laughed at this and his own helplessness, but he spoke with more bitterness of the Tudo's ingratitude, and with some indignation and misplaced vanity of the Liberals depriving him of the title Generalisimo, or at least of Captain-General, he being, he said, in fact the oldest Captain-General of Spain. He said that in the subsequent volumes of his memoirs, he should draw a contrast between Spain under Charles IV., and Spain under the Liberals. He had no great complaint of Napoleon; he had always been his enemy, and Napoleon had offered him fair terms of reconciliation, if he had thought it either honorable or possible to have accepted of them. In his intercourse with him at Bayonne, he had indeed attempted to seduce or intimidate him into a recognition of Joseph, or either then or subsequently in conversation had told him, that from a further knowledge of Spain he had discovered that "l'on l'avoit trompé à son égard;" for that a man could not for near twenty years have governed by his own authority a country composed of such a variety of institutions, of passions, of languages, races, habits, and views as he now found Spain to be, without being a remarkable man. He said that Lucien, with whom he was once intimate, had somewhat unkindly declined all intercourse with him, because, as Lucien said, he had not *ménagé* (he pronounced it *ménassé*) the Emperor in his memoirs. The Prince of the Peace observed that it was no business of his to exalt or to censure Napoleon; it was notorious that they had few relations, but those of hostility rather than friendship, and that in truth he had recounted those affecting Napoleon's conduct without passion, and with a greater disposition to soften rather than to heighten such passages as might lead to unfavorable interpretations. I seized this opportunity of observing that his memoirs were generally, and I supposed with reference to Bonaparte as well as others, more open to the reproach of being either too laudatory or too scrupulous and official in relating facts injurious to the memory of the actors, than to that of calumny and asperity, and I ventured to add that they had lost some of the interest he might have given to them by his relating rather than explaining public acts and documents; whereas in the Court of Spain he must have witnessed scenes, such as would have made the fortune of any memoir writer *à la Française.* I asked if the story of the long period between the celebration and consummation of Ferdinand's marriage was true: he nodded an assurance of its authenticity, but did not dwell on the subject, or even on that of Ferdinand's conspiracy at the Escurial, of which Charles IV. had given me such curious details. He said that I was right in supposing that his great delicacy had diminished the interest taken in his book, and injured the sale; that he thought he should be less fastidious in the volumes on which he was now occupied; that he had not come to the insurrection of Aranjuez, but it would be in the next or following volume. He spoke with less bitterness of Ferdinand, and with more of Don Carlos, than I expected. He acquiesced, indeed, in the somewhat unmeasured epithets with which I stigmatized Ferdinand's character and conduct; but when I said that *celui-ci,* meaning Carlos, though a *dévot* and a bigot, was "plus honnête homme," he said, How can any man deserve the title of "honnête," who would be ready, at the dictation of any silly or wicked beast of a priest or friar, to stab his best friend, or to carry a torch to light a pile to burn father, mother, brother, wife, child, or all his dearest connections? He might not think this dishonest or wrong, but all that the world more justly dreaded or hated, he had the faculty of thinking right, and to the utmost of his power of carrying into execution. He said Spain was in a dreadful condition; that Don Antonio de M——, a man of worth and letters, whom I had known at Madrid, had lately written him word that there was no law, no authority, no safety in the country; and that though he knew of no prohibition against his (the Prince of Peace's) return, he could not say that it would either be prudent or according to law that he should do so, and that even if there were a positive law to say he might, he did not know how he could avail himself of it with any security, or what road he would advise him to take. He said he had been reduced to great distress and degradation; but I found his spirits less depressed and his conversation more natural and frank than I expected. I asked if he saw Don Francisco, and his manner of saying "no" convinced me that that Prince, who is notoriously his son, had made no advances to him, for he somewhat earnestly explained that it did not become him to seek his protection, and enlarged on the opportunities he had of knowing the Infanta before her marriage at Rome, and talking of the beauty of her mother, Isabella, Queen of Naples, who was in all senses, I believe, the own sister of her son-in-law, Francisco.

Soon after he left me, I met on the landing-place of the hotel stairs a dark and somewhat stately lady, evidently of a southern climate, carried by two or three servants on a footstool to the story above our apartment, and, on inquiry, I found it was the Duchesse de Ineca (at least so called), who is the daughter of the Prince of the Peace, and issue of his marriage with the Bourbon Infanta and Princess, and who, as above related, possesses no inconsiderable portion of his landed property. But she neither allows him a sixpence out of them, or keeps up any intercourse with him. She is married to a Roman prince; but his royal consort's children and connections seem to treat him with the same insensibility, harshness, and cruelty as his mistress and wife, the Tudo, and all that depend on her. She is living in comparative splendor at Madrid, while her husband is training a miserable existence as a pensioner or almost beggar in Paris, surrounded by relations, acknowledged or unacknowledged children, grandchildren, and what not—Infants, Princesses, Duchesses, etc., etc., not one of whom condescends to take the slightest notice of him, or show the least tenderness, regard, or interest about one to whom some owe their station and riches, and all, more or less, their very existence! A strange name and fate

"To point a moral or adorn a tale."

No. III.

(See page 95.)

Godoy, in his "Memorias" (tom. iv. p. 431), has inserted both letters, as follows:

Copia literal de la carta que me dirigió Lord Holland despues del fallecimiento de Cárlos IV.

Excelentísimo señor y muy estimado amigo,

Al punto que supe el triste acontecimiento que nos han comunicado los papeles y recientes noticias de Roma, me acordé de la conversacion que tuvimos la última vez que tuve el honor de verle en Verona, y me fuí á ver á los ministros á fin de informarme de si pondrian dificultad en que V. tomase su residencia aquí, en caso de que lo juzgase conveniente. De resultas tengo la satisfaccion de asegurarle que no pondrán impedimento alguno ni á su desembarque ni á su permanencia aquí. No me han dado por escrito esta su determinacion, porque no quieren que semejante paso pueda mirarse como una especie de convite hecho á V., sino como una contestacion sencilla á una pregunta hecha por un amigo, que por tal me hacen el honor de contarme.

Por lo demas, si V. lo juzgase conveniente, puede sin reparo alguno venirse á Inglaterra, adonde vivirá sin sufrir molestia alguna, como otro cualquier extrangero, aunque bajo una ley que da poder á nuestros ministros á obligar á cualquiera de ellos á salir del reino, si asi lo considerasen necessario á la quietud pública. Pero esta ley, puede V. estar cierto que no será usada por ninguna preocupacion nacida de acontecimientos políticos ya pasados. Nuestros ministros tienen empeño en manifestar que no la emplean contra ninguno que no se mezcla en negocios políticos, y como me aseguran que no pondrian ningun impedimento á su disembarque, estoy certísimo de que la tal ley no perturbará su quietud cuando se halle en este pais.

Aunque nada sé de sus planes y determinacion de V. para lo porvenir, me ha parecido que acaso le será á V. útil el saber que en cualquier acontecimiento tiene V. un asilo abierto en este pais. Ojalá que nada adverso le obligue á V. á ello! Pero en cualquier caso, tendré la satisfaccion de haber cumplido con un deber de gratitud por las atenciones que he debido á V., y especialmente por la generosa clemencia con que, en 1805, á instancia mia, salvó V. la vida del infeliz Powell. Este favor está tan vivamente impreso en mi memoria, que no puedo menos de aprovecharme de la primera ocasion que se ofrece, para mostrar mi agradecimiento. Con sinceros deseos de la felicidad de V. quedo su obligado y fiel amigo,

Q. S. M. B.
V. Holland.

En Londres, 30 *de enero de* 1819.

P. D. Una carta dirigida à *Holland House, Kensington, London*, me halla siempre.

Copia literal de mi respuesta.

ROMA, 24 *de febrero de* 1819.

Milord y mi muy amado amigo,

La carta con que V. me favorece de 30 de enero es la mayor preuba de su amistad y la mas relevante demonstracion de la grandeza de su alma. Si, amigo mio, puedo con verdad y con razon querellarme de los hombres, asegurándole que entre el número inmenso de personas á quienes he rendido servicios singulares, una sola no he encontrado que haya correspondido á los sentimientos de nobleza que distinguen al hombre honrado del débil; todos, todos han enmudecido al verme perseguido por la suerte, y solo han recurrido á mí los que necesitaban nuevos socorros de mi liberalidad; este es el mundo, y tal lo conocia; pero la prueba ha sido cruel. Puedo no obstante lisonjéarme de poseer un bien singular, ya que el respetable milord Holland me dispensa su amistad; agradezco pues amado amigo, todo cuando ha ejecutado luego que llegó á su noticia la última desgracia que me aflige, y si las circunstancias del dia no variaren mi suerte mejorándola, seguiré el camino que mi amigo me ha franqueado; seré feliz si algun dia puedo á viva voz demostrarle mi gratitud, y entre tanto concluyo asegurándole la sincera amistad y respeto de su afectísimo servidor,

Q. L. B. L. M.
El Príncipe de la Paz.

No. IV.

(See page 124.)

The following is the copy of an anonymous letter addressed to Lady Holland, to announce the death of Napoleon:

Bonaparte est mort le 5 Mai d'un abcès à l'estomac; la nouvelle officielle en est arrivée aujourd'hui.

Ce 5 Juillet, 1821.

Addressed outside "LADY HOLLAND."

No. V.

(See page 134.)

The following nine letters, referring to the circumstances connected with the imprisonment of Napoleon at St. Helena, are here inserted in their order of date.

My Lord,

C'est vers vous que la justice et l'infortune doivent tourner leurs regards quand elles ont besoin d'un noble appui; j'étais auprès de l'Empereur Napoléon lorsque vous élevâtes la voix dans votre Parlement pour réclamer au nom de l'honneur de votre nation ce que l'humanité, ce que le droit des gens auroient dû prescrir aux ministres de Sa Majesté Britannique; elle retentit jusqu'à lui cette voix généreuse, et porta dans son cœur les plus douces consolations. Puis-je me flatter que ces mêmes ministres accueilliront la demande que j'ai été chargé de faire pour obtenir le remplacement de Monsieur de Montholon, dans le cas prévu alors et réalisé depuis, où sa santé l'obligeroit à quitter l'Empereur? La chance la plus favorable pour moi est de compter sur votre intervention. Lorsque j'ai quitté Ste Hélène, Monsieur de Montholon était comme moi attaqué de la maladie du foie qui me forçoit à m'en éloigner. Son dévouement pour l'Empereur l'a seul empêché de me suivre; mais ce que je craignois est arrivé; il m'écrit que son mal s'est accru, et qu'après avoir fait usage des remêdes les plus énergiques, son état est devenu si alarmant que sans un prompt retour en Europe, ses jours sont dans un imminent péril; mais comme il lui serait pénible de quitter celui, à qui il est devenu necessaire, sans avoir la certitude d'être remplacé par quelqu'un qui fut en état de se livrer aux occupations du cabinet, il me renouvelle les ordres que j'avais dêjà reçus à cet égard. Parmi les personnes nouvellement arrivêes à Longwood, aucune n'est en état d'écrire le François qu'elles parlent à-peine; l'Empereur a absolument besoin d'un homme qui non seulement ait sa confiance, mais qui sache le comprendre. C'est la seule consolation qui lui reste, et il n'est que trop à craindre que de long temps il ne lui en soit accordée d'autre. C'est afin d'obtenir pour cet homme destiné à des titres si délicats, si importans, les permissions nécessaires que je me suis adressée à Lord Bathurst; je n'ai pas essuyé de refus: mais il ne s'est point expliqué sur ma demande que j'avais comprise dans d'autres objets sur lesquels il m'a répondu. Si son silence devait m'annoncer l'intention de l'écarter, j'ose compter sur vous, My Lord, pour la faire sortir de l'oubli auquel il l'aurait condamnée. Dans un pays où l'autorité des ministres est soumise à l'opinion publique, où de respectables organes de cette opinion peuvent leur demander compte de leurs actes si le ministère se tait, il est doux d'avoir la certitude que les amis de la patrie, les honorables soutiens de la gloire Britannique ne se tairont pas; et sur qui cette confiance peut-elle mieux se reposer que sur Lord Holland?

J'ai l'honneur d'être, My Lord, votre très humble et très obéissante servante,

VASSAL DE MONTHOLON.

BRUXELLES 31 *Janvier*, 1820.

STANHOPE STREET, *February 15th*, 1820.

MY DEAR LORD,

If I thought that Count Montholon's life depended upon his departure from St. Helena, and his departure on some person proceeding from Europe to replace him, you will, I hope, do me the justice to believe that there must have been a very cogent reason indeed to have made me doubt of giving my consent. But the fact is, I do not think that his departure depends on this. There is nothing in the various communications which have passed on the intended departure of Count Montholon, which shows it. Even if he had decided not to leave St. Helena until a secretary should be about the person of Bonaparte, the object is accomplished. The priest sent out was selected by Cardinal Fesch, according to the instructions given to his Eminence by Bonaparte for the selection of his priest, and these instructions were, as you may imagine, more particular as to his civil, than to his religious qualifications.

I believe this application of Madame Montholon to be nothing but (to use a very vulgar expression) a mere fetch, more connected possibly with the opposition between Bertrand and Montholon (for we two, my dear Lord, are not I hope half so bitterly opposed to each other) than with any thing else.

What I will do, however, will be this: I will write to Sir Hudson to communicate to Bonaparte that if he shall express any wish for any person from Europe to replace either of these gentlemen (for they are both in fact upon the wing, but watching each other), Cardinal Fesch or the Princess Borghese shall be employed in the business.

I am ever yours, my dear Lord, very sincerely,

(Signed) BATHURST.

I must leave it to you to give the substance of my letter to Madame Montholon, in a way not to offend her. She is, I believe, a very clever woman.

LONGWOOD, *le* 2 *Septembre*, 1820.

MILORD,

J'ai eu l'honneur de vous écrire le 25 Juin 1819, pour vous faire connaître l'état de santé de l'Empereur Napoléon, attaqué d'une hépathie chronique depuis le mois d'Octobre 1817.

A la fin de Septembre dernier est arrivé le Docteur Antomarchi, qui lui a donné des soins; il en a d'abord éprouvé quelque soulagement; mais, depuis, le docteur a déclaré, comme il résulte de son journal et de son bulletin, que le malade est venu à un état tel que les remèdes ne peuvent plus lutter contre la malignité du climat, qu'il a besoin des eaux minérales, que tout le temps qu'il demeure dans ce séjour ne sera qu'une pénible agonie, qu'il ne peut éprouver de soulagement que par son retour en Europe, ses forces étant épuisées par cinq années de sejour dans cet affreux climat, privé de tout, en proie aux plus mauvais traitemens.

L'Empereur Napoléon me charge de vous demander d'être transféré dans un climat européen, comme le seul moyen de diminuer les douleurs auxquelles il est en proie. J'ai l'honneur d'être, Milord, de votre Excellence.

Le très humble et obéissant serviteur.

Le Compte BERTRAND.

P. S. J'avais eu l'honneur d'envoyer cette lettre à Sir Hudson Lowe sous cachet volant; il me l'a renvoyée avec la lettre ci-jointe; ce qui m'engage à vous la faire passer directement. Je suppose qu'il en aura pris copie, qu'il vous l'aura envoyée avec ses observations, et qu'ainsi cette circonstance n'aura occasionné aucun retard.

(Signé) Le Compte BERTRAND.

LONGWOOD, *le* 3 *Septembre*, 1830

S. E. le Lord Liverpool.

(Inclosure in the foregoing letter.)

PLANTATION HOUSE, 2 *Sept.*, 1820.

SIR,

The Governor's instructions not admitting him to receive any letter from the persons residing with Napoleon Bonaparte where the title of Emperor is given to him, I am directed in consequence to return you the inclosed.

The Governor at the same times desires me to observe, that no letter was ever received by him from you, to the address of Lord Liverpool, of the date of 25 June, 1819. I have the honor to be, Sir,

Your most obedient humble servant,

(Signé) G. GORREQUER,
Military Secretary.

Pour copie
(Signé) BERTRAND.

Pour copie conforme,
Princesse PAULINE BORGHESE.

PARIS, *le* 9 *Décembre*, 1820.

MY LORD,

L'intérêt que vous voulez bien prendre au succès de mes démarches relativement à la demande que je fais au gouvernement Anglais d'envoyer un secretaire à Longwood, me fait espérer que je puis sans importunité remettre encore entre vos mains cette cause que je crois juste, et que sans doute le sera à vos yeux.

J'ai l'honneur de vous adresser ma demande à Lord Bathurst; je sais que je ne puis avoir espoir de succès que dans l'intérêt que vous voudrez bien y prendre. Lord Bathurst parait avoir pris contre moi des préventions qui lui font croire que toutes mes demandes cachent quelque mystère inquiétant. Vous serez persuadé, My Lord, que ce n'est pas vous que je voudrais tromper, et que je n'ai qu'un seul but, celui d'apporter quelque consolation au malheur.

Je n'entre vis-à-vis de Lord Bathurst dans aucun détail sur les raisons qui me paraissent devoir être prises en considération; Son Excellence sait mieux que moi que l'on a permis à Napoléon d'avoir trois officiers généraux, plus Monsieur de Las Cases et son fils. M. de Las Cases a été enlevé sans qu'on ait jamais bien compris pourquoi. Le Général Gourgaud a quitté Longwood volontairement. Il ne reste donc plus que deux personnes au lieu de cinq, et je demande d'envoyer M. de Planat comme secretaire de Napoléon. Ce serait ce me semble une barbarie d'exiger qu'il ne partit qu'en remplacement du Comte Bertrand ou du Comte de Montholon. M. de Planat m'a été désigné par l'Empereur comme une des personnes qui lui seraient agréables. On peut même dire qu'il a déjà été choisi par lui puisqu'il l'accompagnoit sur le Bellérophon. Son père était propriétaire à Paris. Il est entré au service en 1806; il a été aide-de-camp du Genl. Lariboissière et du Genl. Drouot; il avait été nommé officier d'ordonnance depuis peu, et n'avait obtenu le grade de chef d'escadron qu'au moment où il a suivi Napoléon; il n'a joué aucun rôle, n'est point exilé, et je ne pense pas qu'il soit suspect au Gouvernement Français. Depuis son retour de Malte, il a toujours vécu en Italie, et est sans fortune, et a reçu un asile auprès de la princesse Eliza (Mme Bacciocchi); il est encore à Trieste.

Son départ me donnera l'espoir du retour de Monsieur de Montholon, espoir auquel je dois renoncer à jamais, si le Gouvernement Anglais refuse la permission d'envoyer un individu qui puisse le remplacer (au moins en partie). C'est assez vous dire, My lord, ce que je vous devrai, et je ne saurais vous exprimer la reconnaissance dont je suis pénétrée pour l'intérêt que vous voulez bien me témoigner, et dont je sens tout le prix.

Lord Bathurst est tombé dans une erreur bizarre sur l'aide de cuisine Pérasset; cuisinier il fût, il est, et il sera vraisemblablement. Ses manières et son langage n'annoncent pas une condition plus relevée.

Je ne veux pas, My Lord, occuper plus longtemps votre attention.

J'ai l'honneur d'être, My Lord, votre très humble et trés obéissante servante,

VASSAL DE MONTHOLON.

A Lord Holland.

VILLA PAOLINA, 29 *Juin*, 1821.

MYLADY,

Sachant par Lord Gower que vous et Mylord êtes à Paris, je profite d'une bonne occasion pour me rappeler à votre souvenir, et vous prier de vouloir bien me donner des nouvelles de mon bien aimé frère, dont l'état de santé m'inquiète beaucoup, par les bruits que l'on fait répandre sur son mauvais état. Nous n'avons reçu aucune nouvelle du prêtre qui est arrivé de Ste Hélène; il vous serait peut-être possible, Mylady, de vous en informer, et de me donner des nouvelles positives.

J'espère que vous êtes satisfaite de votre santé; la mienne a un peu souffert de la mauvaise saison que nous avons ici. Je vous prie, Mylady, de me rappeler au souvenir de Mylord, et de recevoir pour vous l'assurance de mes sentiments d'affection et de reconnaissance, pour toutes les marques d'affection que vous n'avez cessé de donner à mon frère.

Princesse PAULINE BORGHESE.

A Lady Holland.

LONDRES, *ce* 17 *Août*, 1821.

MILORD,

J'ai reçu la lettre que vous m'avez fait l'honneur de m'écrire le 17 de ce mois. J'ai été extrêmement sensible à cette marque de votre intérêt. Je regrette beaucoup que vous avez été absent de ce pays à mon arrivée. Ma première visite eût été certainement chez vous, vous le seul dont la voix se soit élevée dans le Sénat Britannique contre le cruel exil où a péri si malheureusement le grand homme que la France pleurera longtemps. Vous vous êtes acquis, Milord, des droits sur tous les cœurs généreux et à la reconnaissance de tous les amis de l'Empereur. Veuillez me compter parmi ceux qui n'en perdront jamais le souvenir.

Permettez que Lady Holland trouve ici l'expression des sentimens de gratitude que nous devons à la constance de ses soins et de ses attentions pour le proscrit de St. Hélène. Elle a réussi à adoucir les ennuis de son exil; l'arrivée d'une caisse de livres les lui faisait oublier. Tranquille sur le jugement de la posterité, il aimait cependant à retrouver dans les bons ouvrages qu'il était apprécié par ses contemporains, et les libelles lui fournissaient souvent l'occasion d'éclaircir des faits curieux. En un mot, les livres nouveaux étaient pour lui une distraction agréable et un sujet de conversations intéressantes. Le souvenir que l'Empereur a destiné à Lady Holland est conservé avec soin, et lui sera remis par le Général Montholon.

Ma femme se joint à moi pour offrir à Lady Holland ses remerciements des cadeaux, livres, attentions de toute espèce dont elle nous a comblé pendant notre séjour à Ste Hélène. Elle lui écrira pour la remercier de sa lettre, et du logement qu'elle lui destinait à Holland House; comme elle est dans un mauvais état de santé, elle ne compte pas encore quitter Londres.

Veuillez agréer, Milord, les sentimens de haute considération avec lesquels j'ai l'honneur d'être

Votre très humble

et très obéissant serviteur,

Le Compte Bertrand.

The Lord Holland, Paris.

LYONS INN, *Friday*, 17*th January*, 1823.

MADAM,

Not being willing to confide altogether in my own recollection of the substance of the MSS. dictated at St. Helena, I wrote a request to Emmanuel de Las Cases to give me some details upon the subject, especially concerning the volume just published by Colburn. The following is his reply:

"Vous avez raison de penser que le volume des Mémoires '*dictés par lui-même*' est imparfait. Ce sont de simples brouillons que Gourgaud a arrangés et qu'il a vendus. Avec le tems les vrais manuscrits paroitront et feront tomber ce volume. Il y a même deux ou trois additions que l'on a mises pour faire plaisir à certaines personnes.

"Vous avez raison de penser qu'il y avait quelque dissidence entre M. et B.; cependant ils sont toujours bien en apparence, mais ils se fâcheront sérieusement si les mémoires *dictated by himself*, paraissent en totalité; ce dont je doute en ce moment."

The volume of Mélanges consists of extracts from a manuscript brought home by Countess Montholon, and I believe it to be authentic, as far as it goes.

When Gourgaud was on the point of leaving St. Helena, he was required to give up every thing that he had of the dictation of the Emperor, and to pledge his honor that none of it remained in his hands. He gave up some papers, and gave his honor that he had returned all D.; but about three weeks after his departure, it was discovered that he had clandestinely carried off several *brouillons* of Napoleon's dictation, out of which he composed the account which he published of the battle of Waterloo, soon after his arrival in England, and the volume just published.

As I am aware that your Ladyship wishes to obtain authentic intelligence upon what the great Exile has left for posterity, I have done myself the honor to submit the above to you, and have the honor to be, Madam, with unfeigned respect, your Ladyship's very obliged humble servant,

BARRY Q. O'MEARA.

To Lady Holland.

PARIS, 16 *Février*, 1823.

MILORD,

Quoique l'incluse que vous m'avez fait l'honneur de m'annoncer ne se soit pas trouvée dans votre pli, les explications que vous avez eu la bonté de me donner m'ont paru tellement complètes, que je n'ai pas eu à regretter de n'avoir point reçu la lettre de Mr. Fox. Ce que vous me mandez, mon cher Lord, éclaircit autant qu'il était possible la question que j'avais pris la liberté de vous soumettre, et suffit pour tempérer le besoin pressant que je croyais avoir d'une copie figurée du Testament de Sainte-Hélène. J'ai été extrêmement sensible à la peine que vous avez prise de m'écrire entièrement de votre main, et surtout d'une main souffrante. J'aime à me persuader que la douleur est à présent disparue. Peut-être la faveur que vous venez de me faire ne sera pas la dernière que j'aurai à obtenir de vous.

Je désire que la santé de la très aimable Milady n'ait pas été altérée, comme celle du très cher Milord son époux, et je prie le respectable couple d'agréer pour la saanté de l'un et de l'autre les vœux de son dévoué serviteur,

BERTRAND.

P.S. Ma femme est un peu souffrante, et me charge de vous addresser ses compliments affectueux.

Le Lord Holland.

No. VI.

(See page 138.)

The autograph letter to Raynal mentioned in the text is in the British Museum (Egerton MSS. No. xvii.) As it is believed to be inedited, it is now published as it stands in the original.

MONSIEUR,

Il vous sera difficile de vous ressouvenir parmis le grand nombre d'étrangers qui vous importunent de leur admiration, d'une personne à laquelle vouz avez bien voulu faire des honnêtetés. L'année dernière, vous vous entreteniez avec plaisir de la Corse; daignez donc jetter un coup d'œil sur cette esquise de son histoire : je vous présente ici les 2 premières lettres ; si vous les agrées je vous en enverois la fin.

Mon frère à qui j'ai recommandé de ne pas oublier dans sa commission de députés pour reconduire Paoli dans la patrie de venir recevoir une leçon de vertu et d'humanité vous les remetteras.

Je suis avec respect
Votre très humble
et très obéissant serviteur.

BUONAPARTE.
Officier d'Artillerie.

AJACCIO, *le* 24 *Juin, l'an* 1*er de la liberté.*

M. l'Abbé Raynal.

In the "Mémoires" of Lucien Bonaparte, Prince of Canino, Napoleon's brother, occurs the following passage:

"Napoléon, dans un de ses congés qu'il venait passer à Ajaccio (c'était, je crois, en 1790) avait composé une histoire des révolutions de la Corse, don't j'écrivis deux copies, et dont je regrette bien la perte : un de ses manuscrits fut adressé à l'abbé Raynal, que mon frère avait connu à son passage à Marseille. Raynal trouva cct ouvrage tellement remarquable, qu'il voulut le communiquer à Mirabeau. Celui-ci, renvoyant le manuscrit, écrivit à Raynal que cette petite histoire lui semblait annoncer un génie du premier ordre. La réponse de Raynal s'accordait avec l'opinion du grand orateur, et Napoléon en fut ravi. J'ai fait beaucoup de recherches vaines pour retrover ces pièces qui furent détruites probablement dans l'incendie de notre maison par les troupes de Paoli."—Vol. i. p. 92. The autograph of two chapters of Napoleon's history of Corsica is in England, and forms part of the collection of the Earl of Ashburnham.

No. VII.

Letter written to a Lady, in 1832.

DEAR ——,

Why are you so hard upon Louis Philippe? He had the misfortune of being the son of a prince who had little principle and many vices; and whom, from a variety of circumstances, which it would be tedious now to explain, it was and still is the interest and fashion of many factions to blacken and revile far more than he deserved. With all his imperfections in private life, and with whatever delinquencies may be brought home against him in public, he was at heart a most affectionate, indulgent, and judicious father; and that circumstance, combined with his easy and captivating manners, endeared him to all his children, and to none more than his eldest son (Louis Philippe).

Educated in the midst of the revolution, that young prince imbibed popular and even republican principles, distinguished himself in the battle of Jemmappes, fought against the invaders of his country, and with the natural ardor of youth conceived a strong affection and admiration for the general who had led him to victory, and who was in truth no ordinary man—Dumourier. When that general had, partly from the levity of his character, partly from the ill-usage of his employers, deserted the standard of the Republic, and when Egalité the father had, without any proof of guilt, and without any appearance of fear, perished on the scaffold, and his brothers were first imprisoned and then banished, Louis Philippe found himself, without any fault of his own, either through the misconduct of his general, or from the severity of the republican laws, an exile from France; an exile, too, neither welcomed nor protected by the Powers of Europe or the Royalist party, who hated his house and name, and who, moreover, were little disposed to make common cause with any, who were not prepared to invite and carry foreign arms into the heart of their country. To such a line of conduct, which Louis Philippe and his family have uniformly considered as rebellion, he was at this early period of life firmly resolved never to give his sanction. He accordingly entered into no foreign service, accepted no foreign succor of money, except, I believe, some little assistance to his mother, from those courts with which he was connected by blood, and he maintained himself by his industry and proficiency in sciences and arts, which he owed to the provident and careful education, which his father, in the midst of a dissolute life, had always been earnest to procure for him. Surely, thus far, there was nothing to blame in his conduct. Well, in the year 1800, or thereabouts, the state of anarchy in which France was supposed to have wearied out its own partisans, and a notion that something of a more stable, and possibly monarchical nature would be resorted to, was generally prevalent in Europe, and more than whispered in the best informed circles at Paris. But both principle and interest deterred all Frenchmen, who had any value for free institutions, or any concern in the large and extensive purchases of confiscated land, from harboring a thought of bringing back the ancient family, or at least the lineal successors of the last king. Many important personages, however, were suspected, and many actually did look to the *House of Orleans*, as affording a sort of compromise (not very dissimilar to that of William and the House of Hanover in our country), between the bigoted Royalists on one side, and the lovers of liberty on the other. On this occasion, and while speculations of his possible succession to the crown began to be afloat, the Duke of Orleans, at the suggestion of Dumourier, spontaneously recognized Louis XVIII., and reconciled, as far as he could, himself and his family to the exiled dynasty. In taking this step he unquestionably departed in some degree from the principles in which he had started in life. He softened those high, popular, stern, and republican notions which, during the first ardor of the revolution, he, in common with thousands and thousands of enthusiastic young men, had adopted.

Perhaps he did wrong: I think he did; and he seemed, on the score of prudence, to act unwisely; but at least his error, and the season of committing it, bespoke some disinterestedness and generosity. It was the first moment that any prospects of ambition had opened before him, and he renounced them all for the purpose of devoting himself to the cause of persons in adversity, who were indeed related to him, but who, on no one occasion, had ever shown any predilection, and seldom any thing like courtesy or common justice, to him or his family.

It is true, his devotion was neither in profession nor in fact blind or unqualified. He pledged himself to acknowledge no other sovereign of France; he pledged himself to pay allegiance to the heir of the Bourbons, if restored by Frenchmen to the throne of his ancestors; but he did *not* pledge himself to serve or concert with Foreign Powers, for the purpose of forcibly restoring them, and to that reserve and resolution he adhered then, as he has done ever since. It is rumored (and perhaps is true), that in Sicily and at Cadiz he engaged in some intrigues which betrayed the ambition of acquiring political power in Spain, to which his affinity in blood and by marriage gave him some pretension. But what of that? It might be foolish, presumptuous, and adventurous to do so; but it was neither dishonorable, nor unprincipled, nor unjust, nor inconsistent. On the restoration of Lewis XVIII., he returned, consistently with his professions, and in conformity to his interests, to France. The vast possessions of his family fortunately, consisting chiefly in buildings and of forests, had not been sold; they were restored; and they could not on any pretext be withheld. He was moreover admitted as a Prince of the Blood, and a Peer of the House of Peers. His conduct on his return was irreproachable, and in no wise different from that of the Duke of Bourbon, and other Princes of the Blood, but the manner of his reception by the people was very different indeed. It made a much stronger and more lasting impression on the jealous, suspicious, and vindictive tempers of the elder branch of the Bourbons than on his own. He was greeted in the streets and in the Palais Royal with frequent exclamations of "Vivent les Orléans! ah! qu'il ressemble à son bon père! Celui-là n'a jamais porté les armes contre la patrie, nous le sçavons bien." Even before "les cent jours," the Duchess of Angoulême and the Court had begun to mark in trifles, as her mother had done before her, her aversion and spite to the House of Orleans.

It is possible that among the various cabals and intrigues formed by the disaffected during that year, to get rid of the *dynasty imposed upon them by foreign armies*, some may have directed their views to the obvious and reasonable expedient of elevating the House of Orleans to the throne; an expedient analogous to the settlement which had proved so successful in

England. But it was never, I believe, rumored, and certainly never proved, that the Duke of Orleans had, directly or indirectly, the smallest connection or cognizance of any such projects, which, whatever they may have been, were absorbed by the sudden return of Napoleon and his rapid march and occupation of Paris, from whence the House of Bourbon fled as ignominiously, and much more expeditiously, than they had arrived at it. The Duke of Orleans left France too; faithful to his promised allegiance, he did not wait to acknowledge and submit to Napoleon, though such a course held out many obvious advantages, but left his fortune and estates at the mercy of the Imperial government. But though his adherence to Lewis XVIII. withheld him from paying his court to the rival dynasty, it was not sufficient to deter him from his original and laudable resolution of never carrying war into his country. He did *not* go to Ghent. He was no party to any treaty or compact with foreigners, and he retired to Ham, near Richmond, waiting in patience, and some degree of poverty, the event of the contest. When it restored the former order of things, he on permission and invitation returned, though the exclusion of the Princes of the Blood from the right of speaking and voting in the House of Peers (unless specially permitted to do so by the king) was evidently leveled at him; and the whole conduct of the family (the king only excepted) sufficiently indicated that the old enmity to his House was revived, and that nothing but fear and want of power restrained it from breaking out into persecution, or at least perpetual vexation and systematic slander and calumny.

Throughout the reign of Lewis XVIII., though there were many things he disapproved and some he lamented, he never allowed himself to take any active part, nor even encouraged any others to do so. He professed to be under some personal obligation to Lewis XVIII.; and that, and regard to his own honor, utterly prevented him, he said, from any act that could endanger his government, and indisposed him even to such as might embarrass or perplex it.

On the accession of Charles X. that monarch paid him some court, and conferred on him some insignificant favors, but pursued uniformly a system of policy the most adverse to the feelings and principles of the Duke of Orleans, and one which in his judgment led to the catastrophe we have since witnessed, and put, consequently, all princes, and indeed all property, in jeopardy. He concealed his opinions on these matters less, perhaps, than he had done under Louis XVIII., but he neither openly opposed, nor secretly conspired against any; but confined his censures to conversation, and to familiar intercourse with those among the opposition most distinguished *for talent and moderation.* The ordinances came out, and provoked the resistance and revolution of 1830. In preparing that resistance, the Duke of Orleans was never even suspected of taking any share. When the conflict occurred, accidental absence, as well as inclination, kept him aloof; but all parties, *including the King*, began to look to him as the man to whom power (though provisional and temporary) must be delegated for the purpose of restoring tranquillity. The king declared him lieutenant of the kingdom, when in truth he had lost all his own power, and had none to delegate to another; but all the various parties at length acquiesced in the notion of placing him at the head of the country; he was offered the Constitutional Crown, and he accepted it. Could he prudently, could he honestly have done otherwise? If you look to his own honor and engagements, he was as unshackled by any, as any other member of the community; and it was quite clear that, to prevent blood, confusion, and anarchy, some man must be selected. Had he refused, whom would he have benefited? Charles X. and the old Court? Far from it; they would probably have paid the forfeits of their crimes in blood, or at least in imprisonment and confiscation, instead of being allowed, by an act of clemency almost unexampled, to proceed leisurely out of the country, which they had by false oaths deceived, attempted to enslave, and actually deluged in blood, and to withdraw very ample means of subsistence for themselves and the wretched remnant of emigrant rebels, who chose to follow them. The tenderness, perhaps improvident, and certainly almost unprecedented, shown to the exiled family, is mainly to be attributed to the forbearance of Louis Philippe, and to an implied bargain on that subject, which accompanied his elevation to the throne.

Since he was placed there, he has been much ridiculed for a vulgar love of popularity; and yet, whenever the cause of humanity has required it, he has readily and cheerfully risked that darling object without reserve and hesitation. He has done more; he has even put to some peril the confidence of his own party and of the National Guards, for the sake of rescuing from the operation of harsh laws and vindictive policy those who most assuredly would never have shown the same moderation toward him. The escape of Polignac and his colleagues could not but be most unpopular in Paris, where so many parents, widows, and orphans justly attributed the loss of their children, husbands, and fathers to his wicked and sanguinary measures. There can, I think, be little doubt, that, both technically and morally, they had incurred the penalty of treason. Personally, they had no claims whatever on the new king, whose advice they had constantly repudiated, and whose family name and principles they were known to abhor. And yet, at no small hazard to his power, and at yet greater injury to his popularity, he stood forward manfully to screen them from the punishment of death. His whole reign has been marked by similar lenity to his rivals and enemies. He has materially shaken his hold on the country by indulging on all occasions, but especially where the old Royalists are concerned, his natural clemency and good-nature. Compare the proceedings about the infatuated little Duchess of Berry either with those of England toward Charles Edward and the Stuarts, or the conduct of the Courts of Spain, Portugal, and Naples to any competitors or princes engaged in actual hostilities or conspiracies against them. Now, what is there, I ask, in all this to excite indignation?

I have heard some say they do not detest, they despise Louis Philippe. Why, and for what? Not surely for want of talent. If they do, his contemners must be very conceited people, for in knowledge, eloquence, and quickness of apprehension he has not many superiors in Europe. It is not, I presume, for want of courage; for, when in danger, he has displayed much of that essential quality; and he has never, like his predecessors, shrunk from danger, when it in any way became him to encounter it. In the course of this year, on a most trying occasion of an insurrection in Paris (on the 6th of June), he displayed a spirit and presence of mind, a confidence in his own courage, and an intrepidity, which would have done honor to Napoleon himself, and in which it is thought that great man on one or two occasions lost the opportunity of equaling him.

The only contempt really felt for him is for his virtues, *not* his vices; and it is only felt by those who look upon rashness and cruelty as necessary proofs of military and political greatness, and regard all simple in public matters as weakness and pusillanimity. That he has not yet gratified the violent passions of his most zealous partisans, and that he has thereby somewhat deadened their zeal, is most true, and is much to be lamented; but it surely is no ground for the just and impartial to depreciate his character.

So much for his public conduct. Take him in his private capacity, and he is, as a son, a brother, a husband, a father, a master, and a friend quite irreproachable. Easy, good-tempered, good-natured, full of kind affections, and almost exempt from any of the malignant passions, it may be said that with his private character the judgment of the public has nothing to do; but surely it would be dealing but hard measure to the House of Orleans, if the dissolute and unprincipled habits of the father should be deemed sufficient to give currency to the most atrocious calumnies against his public conduct and memory, and yet that the excellent qualities of the son in domestic life should not be allowed to raise a presumption in favor of the motives and principles by which his public actions are regulated.

(Signed) VASSAL HOLLAND.

THE END.

www.ingramcontent.com/pod-product-compliance
Lightning Source LLC
LaVergne TN
LVHW050522100826
845148LV00002B/418